*a* SAVOR THE SOUTH *cookbook*

# Greens

SAVOR THE SOUTH *cookbooks*

*Rice*, by Michael W. Twitty (2021)
*Pie*, by Sara Foster (2018)
*Ham*, by Damon Lee Fowler (2017)
*Corn*, by Tema Flanagan (2017)
*Fruit*, by Nancie McDermott (2017)
*Chicken*, by Cynthia Graubart (2016)
*Bacon*, by Fred Thompson (2016)
*Greens*, by Thomas Head (2016)
*Barbecue*, by John Shelton Reed (2016)
*Crabs and Oysters*, by Bill Smith (2015)
*Sunday Dinner*, by Bridgette A. Lacy (2015)
*Beans and Field Peas*, by Sandra A. Gutierrez (2015)
*Gumbo*, by Dale Curry (2015)
*Shrimp*, by Jay Pierce (2015)
*Catfish*, by Paul and Angela Knipple (2015)
*Sweet Potatoes*, by April McGreger (2014)
*Southern Holidays*, by Debbie Moose (2014)
*Okra*, by Virginia Willis (2014)
*Pickles and Preserves*, by Andrea Weigl (2014)
*Bourbon*, by Kathleen Purvis (2013)
*Biscuits*, by Belinda Ellis (2013)
*Tomatoes*, by Miriam Rubin (2013)
*Peaches*, by Kelly Alexander (2013)
*Pecans*, by Kathleen Purvis (2012)
*Buttermilk*, by Debbie Moose (2012)

*a* SAVOR THE SOUTH *cookbook*

# Greens

## THOMAS HEAD

The University of North Carolina Press CHAPEL HILL

The paper in this book meets the guidelines for permanence and durability of the Committee on Production Guidelines for Book Longevity of the Council on Library Resources.

Cover illustration: © depositphotos.com/brookefuller

Library of Congress Cataloging-in-Publication Data
Head, Thomas, 1942– author.
Greens / Thomas Head.
pages cm. — (A savor the South cookbook)
Includes index.
ISBN 978-1-4696-2668-0 (cloth : alk. paper)
ISBN 978-1-4696-7757-6 (pbk. : alk. paper)
ISBN 978-1-4696-2669-7 (ebook)
1. Cooking (Greens) 2. Edible greens.
I. Title. II. Series: Savor the South cookbook.
TX803.G74H43 2016
641.6′5—dc23 2015029152

*For Mike,*
*my chief culinary adviser and recipe tester,*
*editor, best friend, and husband*

# Contents

*a* SAVOR THE SOUTH *cookbook*

# Greens

# Introduction

*Greens in Southern Culture*

I grew up with turnip greens. Like Sunday school or visits to grandparents, they weren't reserved for special occasions. They were simply part and parcel of a North Louisiana childhood, a culinary and cultural expression of the South.

Greens are an inextricable part of southern culture. In 2011, the Southern Foodways Alliance commissioned "Leaves of Green," a "collard green opera" by Price Walden. The opera contains such memorable lyrics as "From age to age the South has hollered / The praises of the toothsome collard." The collard has been named the state vegetable of South Carolina, and North Carolina is home both to the Latibah Collard Green Museum in Charlotte and to the North Carolina State Collard Green Festival, held each September in Ayden. The festival features a parade, collard-greens-eating contests, and cooking contests. Greens even have been immortalized in country music: Mark Chesnutt, a Texan, says of his ladylove in the song "Daddy's Money," "She's a good bass fisher / A dynamite kisser / Country as a turnip green," while in his song "Good Directions and Turnip Greens," Georgia's Luke Bryan sings of selling turnips from a flatbed truck, and thanks God "for good directions and turnip greens" when the woman of his dreams comes back to him.

Both sets of my grandparents were farmers, and turnip greens were a cold-weather crop that bridged the season between late fall and early spring when little else green was available. My parents brought their parents' style of cooking with them when they moved from smaller towns to Monroe, Louisiana, after my father returned from World War II, and the distinctive fragrance of greens cooking—long and slow—is one of my most vivid memories of my grandmothers' and mother's kitchens.

## COLLARD FESTIVALS

The importance of collards in the culture of the South in general and of the African American community in particular is celebrated in community festivals from North Carolina to California. This list is far from exhaustive, and the dates often change from year to year, so be sure to check with a local source before making plans to attend.

### Ayden, North Carolina

Ayden is home to the Official Collard Festival of the State of North Carolina, held each year on the first weekend in September. The festival includes a pageant, where Miss Ayden is elected, a parade, collard eating and cooking contests, musical entertainment, and carnival rides. This wonderful event shows small-town America going all out to celebrate its local delicacy. For more information, go to www.aydencollardfestival.com.

### East Cleveland, Ohio

The annual Collard Green Cook-Off and Arts Festival here raises money for up-and-coming artists with a contest for the best collards in Cleveland, a fashion show, and sales of food and beverages. The festival is generally held on a Saturday in late September. For more information, go to www.east cleveland.org.

### East Palo Alto, California, and Atlanta, Georgia

The Metro-Atlanta Collard Greens Cultural Festival is an offshoot of the annual festival held in East Palo Alto, California. Founded there by Dr. Nobantu Ankoanda to raise funds for the Shule Mandela Academy, the festival has also been hosted by three different communities in Georgia, most recently Lithonia in DeKalb County. The festival's mission is "to celebrate the traditions, culture and historical contributions of African Americans while promoting family unity and the importance of healthy eating and living for the wellbeing of future generations." And it carries out that mission with gusto: with music ranging from gospel to jazz, an arts-and-crafts marketplace, and programs devoted to healthier cooking. Check www.collardgreensculturalfestival.com for the times and locations of the festivals.

## Gaston, South Carolina
Gaston holds its annual Collard and BBQ Festival around the first weekend in October. There's a parade, a barbecue competition, live entertainment, and free rides for the kids. Check www.gastonsc.org for details.

## Maxton, North Carolina
Held on the second Saturday in November, the Annual Maxton Collard Festival celebrates the culinary heritage of its early settlers, particularly their habit of eating collards with corncakes. Maxton claims to be the collard sandwich capital of the world, and you can compare versions of this delicacy from several vendors. In addition to listening to poems and family stories about collards, you can also enter the collard costume competition. Call (910) 844-5321 for further information.

## Port Wentworth, South Carolina
A festival to celebrate the final harvest and reseeding of the greens is held every year in March at Promised Land Farm in the community of Monteith in Port Wentworth, South Carolina. Events include a parade and a Collards 'n' Cornbread Cook-Off. Go to www.visitportwentworth.com for further information.

For my father, turnips and turnip greens were an essential part of the "vegetable dinner" that was his favorite meal. The rest of the meal, depending on the season, featured some combination of field peas, butter beans, fried okra, fried corn, yellow squash, and sliced tomatoes, and always, cornbread, which was used both as a "pusher" and as a sop for the potlikker that is the delicious by-product of turnip greens. My mother, a dutiful wife of her times, cooked greens for us even though she hated them herself. We kids wouldn't eat turnips, but we loved the greens. Nobody starved.

John Egerton, in his classic book *Southern Food*, claims that turnip greens are most popular in the Upper South and that collard greens are most popular in the lower states. The facts seem to be a bit more complex than that. In their fine book *Collards: A Southern Tradition from Seed to Table* (University of Alabama Press, 2015), Professors Edward H. Davis and John T. Morgan identify a "collard core," comprised of the eastern two-thirds of North and South Carolina, Tidewater Virginia, and northern Georgia, where locals prefer collards to other greens. Davis and Morgan also point to a "collard domain," where collards share popularity with turnip greens and mustard greens. The domain includes parts of nine other southern states: "a small area in southern Arkansas and northern Louisiana, easternmost Louisiana, southern and eastern Mississippi, most of Alabama, northern Florida, and the piedmonts of Georgia, the Carolinas, and Virginia." Turnip greens are the preferred cooked greens in Tennessee, Kentucky, and West Virginia. In a survey of 11,000 college students around the South in which they were asked what greens they preferred, only those in Louisiana reported that they liked mustard greens more than turnip greens or collards.

When I was growing up, my family sometimes had mustard greens instead of turnip greens, which were our favorite, but I have no memory of ever eating collards. My husband Mike is from a different part of the South. His grandfather was a truck farmer in North Carolina and raised various kinds of greens for the local and "Yankee" markets—collards, turnip greens, kale, and Hanover salad—so the pot of simmering greens is also a memory from his childhood. Two of his family's favorite greens dishes were turnips-and-tops and collard greens with cornmeal dumplings, which he always makes for his sister Ann when she visits. I've included that recipe here.

In our house in Washington, D.C., greens still play an important part in our culinary repertoire. When we are dependent on supermarkets, we eat mostly collards, kale, and spinach, the most readily available greens. Turnip greens and mustard greens have also recently become available year-round, but usually in plastic bags, prewashed and chopped. They are usually chopped with their tough central stems, which limits their usefulness, but on occasion, clumsily prepared greens are better than no greens. In the early spring and fall at farmers' markets, we find turnip greens, mustard greens, and other greens you don't usually see at the supermarket like dandelion greens, nettles, lambs quarters, ramps, and beet greens.

Aside from the cultivated varieties of greens, historically, southerners have eaten a great variety of wild greens—poke sallet, dandelion greens, creasie greens, watercress, and many others. For many impoverished southerners, wild greens were an important supplement to their diets.

Because of their color, greens are often associated with money. Traditionally, eating greens with black-eyed peas on New Year's Day is said to bring financial rewards in the coming year. (In North Carolina, a person is said to be guaranteed to earn five dollars in the new year for every collard leaf eaten; in Louisiana, we were always told you'd get a dollar for every black-eyed pea you ate.) Some people believe that a collard leaf hung above a door will keep evil away. Placing a fresh collard leaf on your forehead is a traditional cure for headache. And greens and potlikker have been used as folk remedies for everything from rheumatism to reflux.

In his award-winning book *Soul Food: The Surprising Story of an American Cuisine* (UNC Press, 2013), Adrian Miller points out that greens "have primacy in soul food circles. They are most often the first answer that people will give when asked to name a soul food." Greens were central to the diets of everyone, both enslaved and free, in the South, as culinary historian Leni Sorensen points out. "Everybody gardened. They had to." Rich and poor, black and white, enslaved and free—everybody ate greens because they were easy to grow and, particularly in the South, had a long growing season.

Social, economic, and geographic distinctions often determined what kinds of greens people ate and how they cooked them. In her book *The Virginia House-Wife* (1824), Mary Randolph, Thomas Jefferson's cousin, gives a recipe for turnip tops that are "boiled with bacon in the Virginia style." Adrian Miller gives examples of the slave diet, usually one-pot meals of whatever greens were in season, flavored with a little smoked or salted meat or fish. The children were often given the potlikker.

Another defining characteristic of soul food greens is that they are usually cooked with pork, but Miller points out that this would not have been the case in Africa not only because pork was expensive but also because Africa's large Muslim population would consider consuming it a taboo.

The Spanish explorer and conquistador Hernando de Soto brought pigs to North America, and Sir Walter Raleigh brought pigs to Jamestown from England in 1607. Their numbers quickly grew because they foraged for their own food in the forests and required practically no upkeep. They were rounded up and slaughtered in the fall, and the meat was generally salted or smoked for use during the rest of the year. A fresh pork roast or fresh ham might be a special treat at the plantation Big House for holidays or at pig-killing time, but the usual practice was that all the meat that was not going to be eaten in the next few days went into the salt barrel. It was not until refrigeration became common in the mid-nineteenth century that people bought fresh pork and began to rely on muscle meat.

So pork, or in the coastal regions, smoked or salted fish, became an integral part of the cooking of enslaved African Americans and an essential flavoring ingredient in a pot of greens.

## Origin and History

Collard greens are probably native to the eastern Mediterranean or to Anatolia. The Greeks grew them more than 2,000 years ago, and they were cultivated in Rome in pre-Christian times. The Romans may have brought greens to Britain and France, or the Celts may have already introduced them there. (The word "collard" is Anglo-Saxon in origin, a corruption of "colewyrt," meaning cabbage.)

It is frequently asserted that enslaved Africans brought their taste for greens with them when they were brought to the New World, but greens had been a part of the European diet for at least 2,000 years. When the European slave traders went to West Africa and then came to the Americas, they brought their greens with them. So greens existed in the New World before slavery, but enslaved Africans may also have brought seeds with them. Both local greens and greens imported from Europe were already an important part of the West African diet, and stews of greens and a little bit of meat or smoked fish were a typical meal.

Collards, at any rate, found a comfortable home in the American South. The region's long growing season and mild winters made collards almost a year-round crop, providing nutrition and a green vegetable during the winter months. Greens raised in the "provision grounds," the plots allotted to the slaves for their own gardens, provided not only a valuable nutritional supplement to their diets but also, in some cases, a means for them to earn extra money by selling their produce to the Big House. (Jefferson's granddaughter Anne Cary Randolph kept a careful record of the produce she bought from the slaves at Monticello.)

The turnip is an ancient vegetable and grows wild in Europe and west Asia, along with its relatives, mustards and radishes. It was probably domesticated in that area. There is evidence that turnips were grown for their oil-bearing seed in India before 1500 B.C. Both the Greeks and the Romans grew turnips for food and for livestock fodder. They were widely raised in England for fodder and were brought to the New World in the mid-1600s.

Mustard is believed to have been grown and eaten in the Himalayas for more than 5,000 years. There are more than forty species of mustard plant, many grown for their seeds. The leaves of the plant, mustard greens, play a prominent role in many cuisines, including those of India, Japan, China, Africa, South America, and, of course, the southern United States.

## Nutrition

In a rare conjunction of good taste and good sense, cruciferous vegetables, including greens, are the rage among both chefs and nutritionists these days. Broccoli and Brussels sprouts are almost as common on menus as green beans were just a couple of decades ago. And it's rare to find a southern menu without at least one preparation of greens.

Our ancestors seem to have been aware of the nutritional benefits of eating greens. Nutritional analysis has confirmed this folk wisdom. Greens are often spoken of as "nutritional power-houses," rich in vitamins, minerals, and antioxidants. Like other cruciferous vegetables, collard greens (*Brassica oleracea*), mustard greens (*Brassica juncea*), and turnip greens (*Brassica rapa*) are low in calories and good sources of vitamin C and fiber and are said to have anticancer properties. In addition, collard greens have substantial amounts of vitamins A, K, and many of the B-complex minerals. Turnip greens also have substantial amounts of vitamins A, K, and C, and their somewhat bitter taste is linked to their high calcium content. They also offer antioxidant and anti-inflammatory benefits, and because of their high foliate content, they are thought to offer cardiovascular support as well. Mustard greens offer similar health benefits and are so efficient at absorbing minerals from the soil that they are sometimes grown to cleanse polluted land. (In these cases, the greens are not eaten and must be disposed of safely.)

## Cultivation

Leni Sorensen says that her father, a southerner transplanted to California, claimed that there were two sure ways to tell that people didn't know anything about eating: (1) if they used white cornmeal for cornbread, and (2) if they didn't know how to grow greens. In less than a century we've gone from a time when almost everyone had a vegetable garden to a time when very few people do. Greens figured in most vegetable gardens, particularly in the South. The mild winters of the South made them a source of green vegetables when little else was available, and a farmer could easily harvest two crops a year, once in the spring, and then in the fall. Greens are cold-hardy plants. For an early spring crop of greens, southern farmers often prepare the soil in late fall. They then sow the seeds or plant the seedlings as early in the spring as possible, even before the last frost. These early spring greens, tender and mild in flavor, are particularly prized for the table. Once the heat hits them, they tend to get bitter and quickly go to seed.

For a fall crop, a gardener should sow greens in late summer. Mustard and turnip greens have a growing period of 45–50 days, and collards about 60 days (but they can be eaten before that as baby greens). You may, in fact, harvest collard greens leaf by leaf from the bottom of the plant as they reach the stage of maturity you prefer. You can continue to harvest them well after frost has arrived. In fact, many cooks feel that collard greens are best after the first frost.

There are many varieties of greens—some sprout faster than others, some are more cold resistant, and some are bred for their resistance to pests. Certain varieties of turnip greens yield more plentiful greens than others, and some produce bigger turnips. Mustard greens come in green and red varieties. For most of us, the best guide to what to use is our personal preference and what's available in the markets.

Those of us who cannot grow our own greens are dependent on supermarkets and farmers' markets for them. Turnip greens often come with turnips attached. Look for greens that are crisp, deep green, and free from insect holes or brown edges. Store the greens and turnips separately in plastic bags. They should easily keep fresh for four or five days in the refrigerator. Mustard greens should look fresh and crisp without yellow or brown spots. Store them in the refrigerator like turnip greens. Collard greens are somewhat hardier than mustard or turnip greens. Wrap them, unwashed, in damp paper towels, and store them in the refrigerator, where they should stay fresh for about five days. Wash them thoroughly before cooking them.

## *Traditional Southern Greens*

"Greens!" exclaimed Eugene Walter. "A humble and constant presence in any account of food in the South." "Is there more than one way to cook them?" is the question I've been asked most often when I've told southern friends I was working on this book. My answer is this: There is a traditional southern way of cooking greens, but there are almost infinite variations in ingredients and methods. I've found, however, that five common elements figure into nearly every recipe for traditional southern greens.

1. *Wash the greens.* This might seem to go without saying, but greens grow close to the earth, so they are often dirty and attract bugs and worms, and few things detract more from the pleasure of a pot of greens than biting into grit or finding the remains of insects. Thorough washing is particularly important for greens that you pick yourself from the garden or for greens that you buy from farmers' markets. My method for washing greens is first to rinse them under cold running water in the sink. Then I cut them into whatever size the recipe requires, put them into the basket of a salad spinner filled with cold water, swirl them around with my hands, pour out the water and spin them dry. I might repeat this procedure two or three more times until there is no dirt at the bottom of the spinner.

   These days you can buy bags of prewashed greens in the grocery store, and they are a time saver, but they are usually just chopped, stems and all, so they don't cook as evenly as greens you wash and stem yourself.
2. *Stem and chop the greens.* Most mature greens will have a tough center stem that needs to be removed so that the greens will cook evenly. Working with one leaf at a

time, spread them out on a cutting board, and cut along either side of the center stem. You can either discard the stems, or, as some thrifty cooks do, cook them for a half an hour or so before you add the greens.

3. *Cook the greens with pork.* Cooking greens with pork is a practice that goes back at least to Roman times. They are prepared this way in northern European countries and in the southern United States, of course. Granted, they can be prepared lots of different ways, but for most southerners, pork and greens have a natural, and traditional, affinity. Before the advent of refrigeration, fresh pork was not available year-round, so it was preserved by salting or smoking. Southern cooks added this to a pot of greens both for flavor and for additional protein. Today, lots of different kinds of pork and pork products can be used:

✳ *Smoked pork.* The classic southern way of preparing greens is with smoked pork, either cooked with the greens or used to make a rich stock in which the greens are then cooked. A ham hock is the most usual form of smoked pork for greens. It requires long cooking to become tender, and when the greens are finished cooking, the skin and bones of the ham hock are often removed from the hock, the meat is chopped, and then it's added back to the greens. Almost any kind of smoked pork can be substituted for the ham hock, though—bacon, neck bones, even a glug of bacon grease from the "fried meat grease" can that resides at the back of many southern stoves. Many people these days cook their greens with smoked turkey parts to reduce the fat, but I don't think smoked turkey is nearly as flavorful as smoked pork.

✳ *Salted pork.* Along with cornmeal, salt pork, or in coastal regions smoked fish, was often part of the "customary" given to enslaved Africans. The kinds of salted pork available to us today include side meat, pork belly, and fatback. All can be used to cook greens, but it's often a good idea to blanch it before using it in recipes to get rid of excess salt. I occasionally cure pork belly with salt and herbs and sometimes smoke it after curing it for several days in the refrigerator. It's great cooked with greens or as an accompaniment to them.

* *Ham.* Hams are cured either by smoking or by salting. Ham bones or ham scraps are frequent leftovers in our kitchen. Even commercial hams add good flavor to a pot of greens, but country ham or country ham scraps are even better. I've also cooked greens with tasso, the spicy Cajun ham, when I've had it.

Although it is traditional to cook greens with pork, times are changing. Adrian Miller points out that in soul food restaurants, even those in the Deep South, "pork is no longer the default seasoning for vegetables." There are many reasons for this change—health consciousness, vegetarianism, veganism, and religious taboos against eating pork. The downside of this trend, Miller reports, "is that quite a few places have cut out the pork but aren't doing much else to season their greens. I think they're relying on [patrons] to make up the difference with a dash of hot sauce or vinegar."

4. *Cook in lots of liquid.* It may be traditional to cook greens in water, but cooking them with chicken stock, homemade or canned, gives an additional layer of flavor. Ham stock (page 23) obviates the need for additional flavorings. You can also use vegetable stock, but I find that the strong flavors of the greens overpower any additional flavor that the stock might give.

The wonderful side product that comes from cooking greens with water or stock is potlikker, which is as much a southern tradition as the greens themselves (see page 41).

5. *Flavor with vinegar.* Adding a bit of acid to brighten up the flavor of a pot of greens is a traditional southern practice. In the traditional kitchen, vinegar, which was readily available and shelf-stable, was the ingredient of choice. Today's cooks often add a squeeze of lemon, which seems to have a greater affinity for quickly sautéed greens.

6. *Season with hot pepper.* It's a common practice when cooking traditional southern greens to throw a hot pepper or a pinch of dried red pepper flakes into the pot. You can add acidity and a bit of heat to the greens at the same time by sprinkling a dash of pepper vinegar at the table. A jar of this ubiquitous southern condiment, either homemade or commercially prepared, often sits on tables beside the salt and pepper both in homes and at restaurants. It's also tasty on barbecue, in a spicy vinaigrette, or even in a bloody Mary.

## New Southern Cooking

Influenced by time constraints, health concerns, and the foodways of new immigrant groups that have found a home in the South in recent years, a new generation of southern chefs and home cooks have taken the traditional dishes of the South and adjusted them for today's ways of cooking.

These days, few families have time to simmer a pot of greens on the stove for two hours when most mothers and fathers who share the cooking responsibilities have jobs outside the home and are faced with getting dinner on the table after a full day's work. One technique that has emerged for cooking greens faster is to let the knife do the tenderizing—to chop or shred the greens so that they cook more quickly. Another is to use the slow cooker to cook greens slowly all day and have them hot and tender by dinnertime—a convenience our grandmothers would never have dreamed of.

A new appreciation for the distinctive qualities of individual greens and their cultivars has encouraged chefs and home cooks to treat each type of green individually and with respect. Early spring greens, which are more tender and milder in flavor than fall greens, are often eaten raw or lightly sautéed, sometimes in butter rather than pork fat. Fall greens are often cooked with pork, chicken, or ham stock and flavored with hot sauce, vinegar, or pepper vinegar.

Many imaginative southern cooks have come up with ways of incorporating greens into southern-style dishes in which they were not traditionally used. Some examples include Birmingham, Alabama–based chef Frank Stitt's collard green and white bean gratin, author and television cooking show host Nathalie Dupree's grits and greens, Alabama-born chef Scott Peacock's spicy collards in tomato-onion sauce, and New Orleans–born chef John Currence's collard choucroute garni. These greens variations on southern themes are an important part of restaurant cooking in the twenty-first century and offer new possibilities for the home cook as well.

Southern cooks have also been busy exploring the multicultural influences on southern cooking, including those of the new immigrant communities that have lately flourished in the South. In 2010, the Southern Foodways Alliance sponsored a symposium titled "The Global South." Sandra Gutierrez talks deliciously about the affinities between southern and Latino cooking (that of the South's largest recent ethnic group) in her book *The New Southern Latino Table* (UNC Press, 2011). And Paul and Angela Knipple's *The World in a Skillet* (UNC Press, 2012) shows how first-generation immigrants have transformed southern food culture by cooking their native dishes with traditional southern ingredients.

During my years as a restaurant reviewer, I was delighted to discover that the greens that I loved in the South were also popular in the Caribbean, South America, Asia, and Africa. In the Mediterranean, where they were traditionally gathered wild, they are now often available in markets.

In the Caribbean, greens are often flavored with lime juice or coconut milk, with turnip greens or mustard greens substituting for the favored callaloo. In Brazil, collard greens are an indispensable part of *feijoada*, that elaborate special-occasion feast of beans and pork parts. In West Africa, the region from which Africans probably brought collards to the Americas, a wide variety of greens is cooked in stews, with fish, and in combination with other vegetables. In Indian and Ethiopian cuisine, greens are often cooked with a variety of spices such as cumin and cardamom instead of the smoked meat common in the United States. Asian cuisines such as Chinese and Thai have their own panoply of greens, but common American varieties can often be substituted to good effect.

When I have traveled in Italy and France, I saw how both countries delight in the bitter greens that were traditionally foraged in the early spring but are now often available in markets. The most tender of them are eaten raw in salads. In Italy, older or tougher greens are cooked and eaten with a little olive oil or blanched and added to pasta sauces, soups, and stews, and in France, they are often incorporated into a gratin or a soup.

As a food writer and former restaurant reviewer, I'm often asked, "What is your favorite kind of food?" It's an easy question for me to answer. While I love Italian and French cooking and delight in Chinese, Japanese, and Thai food, there's nothing I like better than the southern cooking I grew up with. When I visit relatives back in Louisiana, they often apologize for serving me a "plain country meal." This "simple" country meal might consist of fried chicken, chicken and dumplings, fried corn, long-cooked green beans, fresh sliced tomatoes, cornbread, and if I'm really lucky, a big pot of turnip greens in potlikker. This food means home and security and comfort to me. I'm delighted greens are healthy; I'm happy greens have become fashionable. But I eat them not because they are good for me but simply because that hot, dark green potion is part of who I am.

# The Basics

"The way my grandmother taught me to make collards is very simple. The idea is to boil the hocks until they begin to fall apart. Since this is a lot of collards, you will need to add them until the pot is full. Then allow them to wilt as they cook—then add more. . . . Cook on medium heat. Taste to confirm they are the tenderness that you prefer."—from *Leaves of Greens: A Southern Oratorio in 3 Parts*, by PRICE WALDEN.

# Basic Southern Greens

*Although this book aims to demonstrate the versatility of greens, most of us who grew up in the South ate them cooked only one way—simmered in water with smoked pork. Some people add onions, garlic, red pepper flakes, and vinegar for extra flavor, so I've given instructions for both methods here. You can use this basic recipe in many of the recipes in this book that call for cooked greens.*

MAKES 8 SERVINGS

---

2 pounds greens (collards, mustard greens, turnip greens, beet greens, kale, or a combination)

1 pound ham hocks or other smoked meat (neck bones, smoked turkey, etc.) or 6 strips thick-sliced bacon, cut into 1-inch pieces

Water or chicken stock

$\frac{1}{2}$ teaspoon crushed red pepper flakes (optional)

1 cup chopped onion (optional)

2 garlic cloves, put through a press (optional)

2 tablespoons vinegar (optional)

Salt, to taste

---

Cut out the thick, tough center stems of the greens and discard; cut the leaves into roughly 2-inch-square pieces. Wash the greens thoroughly in at least two changes of cold water (I usually do three). Drain in a colander.

Unless you are using the optional ingredients, combine the greens and meat in a large pot and add enough water or chicken stock to cover them. Bring to a boil and simmer until the greens are tender (anywhere from $\frac{1}{2}$ hour for young greens to 1 hour for older collards).

If using the onion and garlic, in a pan large enough to hold the greens and water, sauté the bacon over medium heat until the fat is rendered but the bacon is not yet crisp. Add the onions and continue cooking until they are translucent but not brown. Mash the garlic into the pan and cook for about 30 seconds, being sure not to let the garlic brown. Add the greens, the red pepper flakes, and enough water to cover the vegetables. Bring the liquid to a boil, reduce the heat, and simmer until the greens are tender (see above). Just before serving, stir in the vinegar and season with salt.

## MEASURING GREENS

My mother and grandmothers often talked about fixing a "mess" of greens for dinner. You won't find measuring cups or scales graduated by messes, but when southerners talk about a mess of greens, they mean, roughly, the amount it takes to feed their family.

The fact is that cooking greens is not an exact science. Our ancestors measured by eye, not by cups or ounces. If you have a few more greens, a little less stock, or a slice more or less of bacon than a recipe calls for, your greens dish will turn out just fine.

But in an effort to bring some consistency to these recipes, I've used the following equivalents:

* 1 pound of greens on the stem equals about 8 cups of stemmed and chopped greens
* 2 cups of stemmed, chopped, and cooked greens equal 1 half-cup serving.
* 1 pound of greens serves 4.

# Everyday Cornbread

*"Cornbread and turnip greens, Dixie cup of ol' Jim Beam," sings J. B. Roberts in his song "Outlaws Like Me," evoking two favorites that for most southerners are inevitably combined. We ate cornbread several times a week in the Head house. It was absolutely necessary with greens and the other southern vegetables—purple hull peas and butterbeans among them—that my father was so fond of.*

*The cornbread I grew up with was made with cornmeal from the supermarket, probably Quaker or whatever brand was cheapest. We used white cornmeal, which most southerners seem to prefer, but I really don't think the color makes any difference to the taste of the cornbread. These days there are a number of mills in operation that make old-fashioned stone-ground cornmeal. Anson Mills in Columbia, South Carolina (www.ansonmills.com), has done a wonderful job of seeking out heirloom varieties of corn and making them commercially available. Their cornmeal is coarse and delicious and just tastes more like corn than the commercial varieties, but keep in mind that since stone grinding doesn't remove the germ (as the commercial steel rollers do), the cornmeal is perishable and must be stored in the refrigerator or freezer.*

*When I read the bit of my great-grandfather's diary that survives—he was a farmer in North Louisiana—I wondered why he had to go to the mill to get his corn ground every week or two. That's the reason—the cornmeal didn't last long, particularly in hot Louisiana weather with no refrigeration. That and the fact that most millers were also distillers. I suspect that the mill was where he bought the "O be joyful" that he mentions drinking on several occasions.*

*I used to take it as fact that the difference between southern and Yankee cornbread was that Yankees put sugar in their cornbread and southerners never did until I heard food journalist Toni Tipton Martin speak emotionally at a Southern Foodways Symposium at the University of Mississippi. She pointed out that black* southerners do put sugar in their cornbread and that we shouldn't define southern food by what white people alone do. Another sad example of how we've lived so close for several hundred years and know so little about each other's cultures.

My parents never measured the ingredients for cornbread. This cornbread, my go-to recipe, is a close approximation of theirs. It's based on a recipe from Mildred Swift's book Looking at Cooking. She had a cooking program on KNOE TV in Monroe, Louisiana, when I was growing up, and I still frequently refer to her book for recipes for southern standards.

Every southern family has its own recipe for cornbread. This is the one I use.

I always cooked cornbread in a single "pone" in a ten-inch cast-iron skillet, but a trick I learned from my cousin Emmilee Green is to divide the batter in half and cook it in two skillets. It's thinner this way and has more of the delicious crust that is everyone's favorite part. You can cook cornbread in something other than a well-seasoned cast-iron skillet, but no other pan seems to produce the proper crisp crust.

MAKES 8–16 PIECES

3 tablespoons melted bacon fat (vegetable oil will do
    in a pinch)
1½ cups cornmeal
½ cup flour
1½ teaspoons salt
1 teaspoon baking powder
¾ teaspoon baking soda
2 eggs
1¾ cups buttermilk

Preheat the oven to 425°. Place the bacon fat in a 10-inch cast-iron skillet and put the pan in the oven to heat.

Mix the dry ingredients in a large bowl. Place the buttermilk in a 4-cup measuring cup; beat in the eggs and 2 tablespoons of the melted fat from the skillet.

Make a well in the dry ingredients and pour in the wet ingredients. Mix well.

Pour the batter into the skillet (it will sizzle and immediately begin to cook around the edges) and bake for 20–25 minutes or until the mixture pulls away from the sides of the pan. Turn out immediately onto a platter, bottom side up and slice into wedges.

# Ham Stock

*Along with chicken stock, Mike and I always try to keep a couple
of quarts of ham stock in the freezer. It comes in handy to cook up
a bunch of greens without the need for smoked meat or to use as a
base for sauces that can benefit from the smoked-meat flavor. The
long cooking gives a depth of flavor that is hard to achieve in a
dish of greens without overcooking them.*

### MAKES 2 QUARTS

---

3–4 pounds smoked pork on bones, scrubbed (neck bones,
    hocks, hambone, etc.)

4 medium carrots, quartered

2 celery stalks with leaves, if available, cut into large pieces

1 or 2 bay leaves

5 parsley stems with leaves

8 cups chicken stock

8 cups water, or enough to cover the other ingredients

---

Combine all of the ingredients in a large stockpot and bring
to a boil; reduce the heat and simmer for 1½ hours.

Strain out the vegetables and meat. When the pork is cool
enough to handle, pick the meat off the bones and reserve to
garnish greens or for another purpose.

If desired, skim the fat off the stock. Freeze in 1-quart
containers.

# Hot Pepper Sauce

*A bottle of hot pepper sauce, either bought or homemade, often occupies a place beside the salt and pepper on southern tables. It's an absolute necessity for sprinkling on greens, but it's often used as a condiment for other vegetables or for meat, and is even used as a substitute for ordinary vinegar in salad dressings. It's easy to make and can be made in any quantity in almost any container, from a pint jar or a sterilized catsup or Worcestershire sauce bottle to an elegant cut-glass cruet. I prefer to use a half-pint cruet bottle with a gasket lid. Any kind of fresh chili pepper will work — jalapeño, Serrano, cayenne, or tiny bird peppers, which look especially attractive in the bottle. The acidity brings out the flavor of the greens and the pepper warms the taste buds.*

MAKES AS MUCH AS YOU HAVE ROOM IN A JAR FOR

**Hot peppers**
**White vinegar**

Sterilize a jar by filling it with boiling water; empty the water and let the jar air dry. Wash and stem the peppers and pack them into the jar. Fill the jar with vinegar, cap it, and let stand for 10 days in a cool, dark place before using.

NOTE ✽ If it makes you feel better, you can store the pepper sauce in the refrigerator, but the acidity of the vinegar makes it shelf-stable.

# Appetizers, Soups, and First Courses

It wasn't turnip greens soup that *Alice in Wonderland*'s Mock Turtle had in mind when he sang "Beautiful soup so rich and green, waiting in a hot tureen," but any soup with greens is a great way to start a meal. Southern greens make a good stand-in for spinach or artichokes in dips and crostata toppings, and small portions of greens tarts make great cocktail snacks.

# Cajun Caldo Verde

*This green soup is practically the national dish of Portugal. On its native turf, it's made with a kind of dark green cabbage not easily found in this country and with* linguiça, *a spicy smoked sausage. In this recipe I substitute collard greens or kale for the cabbage, and Cajun andouille is a good, if slightly spicier, stand-in for the Portuguese sausage. Serve with a pone of good old-fashioned southern cornbread.*

MAKES 8 SERVINGS

½ pound Cajun-style andouille, sliced into ⅓-inch-thick rounds

2 medium onions, diced

2 garlic cloves, finely chopped

8 cups homemade chicken stock or commercial reduced-sodium chicken broth

2 pounds Yukon Gold potatoes, peeled and cut into 1-inch dice

1½ teaspoons salt

½ teaspoon freshly ground black pepper

2 pounds collard greens or kale, washed, stemmed, and finely shredded

2 tablespoons fresh lemon juice

Olive oil for drizzling

In a heavy Dutch oven over medium heat cook the andouille until the fat is rendered and it begins to brown. Remove the sausage to a side dish, pour off all but about 2 tablespoons of the fat, and cook the onions until they are tender and translucent but not brown, about 6–8 minutes. Add the garlic and cook until fragrant, about 30 seconds.

Add the chicken stock, potatoes, salt, and pepper. Bring to a boil, reduce the heat to low, and simmer until the potatoes are tender, about 10–15 minutes. Using a potato masher or an immersion blender, mash or purée the soup until it is thick and chunky. Add the sausage and greens and simmer until the greens are tender, about 5 minutes. Stir in the lemon juice, taste for seasoning, and serve, drizzled with a little olive oil, in bowls.

# Collard Greens Empanadas

*My friend Sandra Gutierrez, in her book* The New Southern-Latino Table *(UNC Press, 2011), brings a wonderful Latin American accent to the standard dishes of the southern repertoire. She makes these collard green empanadas for New Year's Day because eating greens on New Year's Day is said to bring luck. They are so delicious that I see no reason to confine them to one day a year. She uses prepared empanada dough cut into rounds that can be found in the freezer section of most Latin markets. Sandra notes that the empanadas can be made ahead of time and frozen, then put directly from the freezer into the deep fryer.*

### MAKES 8 SERVINGS

2 tablespoons vegetable oil or bacon drippings
½ cup finely chopped yellow onion
4 large garlic cloves, finely chopped
10 cups thinly shredded collard greens or kale
½ cup cooked and finely chopped bacon (about 7 slices)
1 (8-ounce) package cream cheese
¼ teaspoon cayenne pepper
16 prepared empanada disks, thawed
Vegetable oil for frying

In a large skillet, heat the oil over medium-high heat; add the onions and cook, stirring often, for 2 minutes, or until they begin to turn golden. Add the garlic and cook for 20 seconds. Add the shredded collards in batches, making sure to stir them quickly, so that the garlic doesn't burn. Reduce the heat to medium-low and cook the collards for 3 minutes, or until wilted; remove from heat and let cool for 10 minutes. In a medium bowl, combine the cooked collards with the bacon and cream cheese; add the cayenne and stir well to combine.

Working on a clean surface, separate the empanada disks (keep them covered with a clean towel as you work, to prevent drying). Place a heaping ¼ cup of the filling on one-half of each disk, making sure to leave a ½-inch rim. Fold the disk in half over the filling and press the edges firmly with the tines of a fork to seal.

Fit 2 large baking sheets with cooling racks. In a large skillet with high sides, heat 2–3 inches of oil to 360° F (or use a deep fryer according to the manufacturer's instructions). Working in batches, carefully slide the empanadas into the oil and fry them for 3–4 minutes, or until golden brown, turning them over halfway through. Use a slotted spoon to transfer the empanadas to the prepared cooling racks. Serve hot.

# Elizabeth Petty's Kale Chips

*Kale chips have become a popular, healthful snack, and recipes for them abound. The tastiest ones I have ever eaten are made by my neighbor Elizabeth Petty, a caterer who also runs an elegant, one-night-a-week raw food restaurant in Washington called Elizabeth's Gone Raw. She serves kale chips as a predinner snack with drinks. So that they will merit the designation "raw," Elizabeth dries her kale chips in a dehydrator at 115°. If you don't have a dehydrator, you can achieve good results by cooking them in a 225° oven.*

### MAKES ABOUT 10 SERVINGS WITH DRINKS

2 pounds kale, washed and patted dry

1 red bell pepper, seeded and diced

1/4–1/2 medium-size jalapeño pepper, seeded and diced

1/4 pound cashew pieces

1 ounce sunflower seeds

3 tablespoons nutritional yeast

1/2 cup water

2 teaspoons sea salt

2 tablespoons fresh lemon juice

3/4 teaspoon cayenne pepper

3/4 teaspoon smoked paprika

Put all the ingredients, except the kale, into the container of a blender (a Vitamix works best). Blend until smooth. Adjust the seasonings as desired.

Massage the cashew mixture into the kale leaves until they are completely coated.

If you have a dehydrator, place the kale on dehydrator sheets in an even layer and leave in dehydrator at 115° for at least 12 hours or until crisp.

If you don't have a dehydrator, preheat the oven to 225°. Line three rimmed baking sheets with parchment paper or Silpat liners. Spread the coated kale pieces in the pans in one layer and bake, rotating the pans occasionally, until crisp, about 1 hour. Store in an airtight container.

# Lebanese Collard and Lentil Soup

*This Lebanese treatment of collards demonstrates the versatility of this leafy green. This low-fat vegetarian soup can be eaten either hot or cold. Accompanied by heated pita or another flatbread, it makes a hearty and healthy lunch. It is worth seeking out red lentils for this soup. They are less likely to turn to mush than the more familiar brown ones.*

MAKES 4 SERVINGS

4 tablespoons olive oil, divided
1 medium onion, chopped
1 carrot, chopped
1 celery stalk, chopped
1 small green bell pepper, chopped
4 garlic cloves, finely chopped
1 cup dried red lentils, rinsed
6 cups water or vegetable stock
1½ pounds collards, washed, stemmed, and roughly chopped
1 tablespoon ground cumin
1 teaspoon ground cinnamon
¼ cup fresh lemon juice
Salt and freshly ground black pepper, to taste

Heat 2 tablespoons of the olive oil in a stockpot or large sauce-pan. Add the onions, carrots, celery, and bell peppers and cook over medium heat until the vegetables are tender but not brown, about 6 minutes. Add the garlic and cook until fragrant, about 30 seconds. Toss the lentils into the pan and stir until they are coated with oil. Add the water or vegetable stock and cook until the lentils are tender, about 15 minutes.

While the lentils are cooking, heat the remaining olive oil in a medium frying pan with a cover. Stir in the collard greens and season with cumin and cinnamon. Cover and cook, add-ing a little water if necessary, until the greens are tender, about 10 minutes.

When the lentils are cooked, stir in the greens and simmer for about 10 minutes to blend the flavors. Stir in the lemon juice and season with salt and pepper.

# Miang Kham

*When I started reviewing restaurants in the early 1990s, there was a place in Old Town Alexandria, Virginia, called Cajun Bangkok that offered both Cajun and Thai cuisine. It's not an outlandish combination—both cuisines depend heavily on seafood and both use hot peppers extensively. Miang kham is a traditional Thai street food in which various condiments—often including ginger, dried shrimp, peanuts, and roasted coconut—are wrapped in a leaf, topped with a tangy sauce, and eaten in a single bite. The traditional Thai version uses wild tea leaves, also called betel leaves, for the green. Cajun Bangkok substituted collard greens to very good effect. A platter of rounds of raw collard greens and small containers of the sauce and the various fillings makes for a delightful, participatory cocktail snack. Each bite contains a delightful combination of textures and sweet, salty, and sour flavors. Dried shrimp, palm sugar, and fish sauce can be found in Asian markets or the Asian food sections of large supermarkets.*

MAKES ABOUT 8 APPETIZER PORTIONS

¾ cup unsweetened shredded coconut

¾ cup raw unsalted peanuts

¾ cup dried shrimp (about 8 ounces), divided

1 tablespoon grated fresh ginger

¼ cup plus 2 tablespoons finely chopped shallots, divided

¼ cup palm or coconut sugar, or 2 tablespoons granulated sugar

2 tablespoons fish sauce (*nahm pla*)

½ cup water

12 collard leaves, each about 7 inches across

6 Thai chilies, sliced into rounds, or 3 Serrano peppers, chopped

1 lime, cut into ¼-inch pieces, each piece containing a
    bit of peel and a bit of flesh

⅓ cup diced fresh ginger

⅓ cup cilantro leaves

To make the sauce, in a small frying pan over medium heat, toast the coconut until it begins to brown. Remove the coconut, add the peanuts to the pan, and roast until they begin to brown.

In a food processor, grind ¼ cup of the shrimp, the ginger, and 2 tablespoons of the shallots; add ¼ cup of the coconut, ¼ cup of the peanuts, the sugar, the fish sauce, and the water and process to a smooth purée. Transfer the mixture to a small pan, bring to a boil, and simmer until slightly thickened, about 10 minutes. Set aside to cool. The sauce, served cold, can be made in advance and refrigerated until ready to use.

Lay each collard leaf on a flat surface; using a 3-inch round cookie cutter, cut circles from the leaves on either side of the center stem and place them on a platter.

To serve, put a bowl of the sauce in the center of a large serving tray. Around the sauce, put piles (or small bowls) of each of the chilies, lime, ginger, cilantro, and the remaining coconut, peanuts, shrimp, and shallots. Each diner takes a collard circle, tops it with her or his desired condiments, tops it with a small amount of sauce, and eats it in one bite.

# Cream of Collard Greens Soup

*The addition of collard greens to a basic leek and potato soup gives it a lovely green color and a pleasant bite that makes it a perfect prelude to a summer meal. Like leek and potato soup, it can be served hot or cold. For an even more robust flavor, use ham stock instead of chicken stock or water, or, for a vegetarian version, use vegetable stock or water.*

MAKES 6 SERVINGS

4 tablespoons butter
4 large leeks, white and tender green parts only,
    thinly sliced
2 garlic cloves, finely chopped
6 cups chicken stock or ham stock (page 23)
1½ pounds small russet potatoes, peeled and cubed
1 pound collard greens, washed, stemmed, and cut into
    thin ribbons
Salt and freshly ground black pepper, to taste
Pinch of cayenne pepper
Chives or ham, finely chopped, for garnish

Melt the butter in a large saucepan over medium heat. Cook the leeks and garlic in the butter until tender but not brown, about 10 minutes. Add the stock, potatoes, and greens and cook until the potatoes are very tender, about 15 minutes.

Purée the soup with an immersion blender or put it through a food mill. Add hot water to reach the consistency you like. Season with salt, pepper, and cayenne. Serve in bowls, garnished with the chives or ham.

To serve cold, let the soup come to room temperature then refrigerate until thoroughly chilled. Garnish as above.

# Mustard Greens Pesto

*Spicy mustard greens make a good substitute for basil in pesto. Serve it before a meal as a dip with corn chips or use it as a pasta sauce. It will keep in the refrigerator for two or three days, and like basil pesto, it freezes very successfully. Add the frozen pesto to hot pasta, and you have a quick, easy meal.*

MAKES ENOUGH PESTO FOR 2 POUNDS OF PASTA

1 pound mustard greens, washed and stemmed
3 garlic cloves, peeled
½ cup freshly grated Parmesan cheese
⅓ cup olive oil
½ cup toasted pecans
½ teaspoon salt
½ teaspoon freshly ground black pepper
Dash cayenne pepper

Blanch the mustard greens in boiling water for about 2 minutes. Drain, cool under running water, and squeeze dry.

Drop the garlic cloves through the feed tube of a food processor while it is running. Stop the processor and add the greens, cheese, and olive oil. Process to a smooth purée.

Add the pecans and pulse 2 or 3 times until the nuts are coarsely chopped. Transfer the pesto to a bowl and add the salt, pepper, and cayenne.

# Mustard Greens Soup

*Scott Muns is* chef de cuisine *at Volt restaurant in Frederick, Maryland. At a recent birthday lunch, I was dazzled by the flavor of his mustard green soup. I asked for the recipe, which he generously shared. What follows is a much simplified version of the restaurant's original recipe but one that is, I hope, faithful to the original flavors. The greens, the soup base, and the mussels can be cooked in advance and combined just before serving. The color is lovely and the flavors are intense. It's a wonderful dish to begin a special occasion dinner.*

MAKES 8 SERVINGS

FOR THE GREENS

1½ pounds mustard greens, washed, stemmed,
    and cut into 2-inch pieces
2 teaspoons salt

FOR THE SOUP BASE

2 tablespoons olive oil
1 large onion, sliced
8 garlic cloves, chopped
½ pound button mushrooms, sliced

FOR THE MUSSELS

2 tablespoons olive oil
6 garlic cloves, chopped
½ small fennel bulb, chopped
Pinch of crushed red pepper flakes
1 bay leaf
5 sprigs parsley
5 sprigs tarragon
1 cup dry white wine

**1½ pounds mussels**
**Salt, to taste**
**Fresh lemon juice, to taste**

---

To cook the greens, bring 10 cups of water to a vigorous boil. Add the salt and mustard greens and blanch them for about 5 minutes. Drain them, reserving the water, and immediately plunge the greens into a bath of ice water. Once they are cold, squeeze out as much water as possible and place them in a blender. Purée until smooth, adding a couple of ice cubes and just enough of the reserved water to allow the blender to do its work. Remove the purée to the refrigerator.

To make the soup base, heat the olive oil in a large frying pan over medium heat. Add the onions and garlic and cook until soft and translucent, about 10 minutes, reducing the heat if necessary to keep them from browning. Add the mushrooms and sweat them for about 10 minutes. Add 5 cups of the reserved water from blanching the greens and bring to a simmer. Cook for 15 minutes. Transfer the contents of the pan to a blender; purée until smooth. Set aside.

To prepare the mussels, in a large pan with a lid, sweat the onion, garlic, fennel, and red pepper flakes in the olive oil over low heat until soft and translucent. Add the herbs and cook for 1 minute. Pour in the white wine and bring to a simmer. Add the mussels, cover, and steam just until they open. Remove the mussels, cool, pull the meat from the shells. Strain the mussel cooking liquid from the solids. Discard the solids and reserve the liquid.

When ready to serve, combine the mussel cooking liquid and the soup base in a medium saucepan. Add enough of the mustard green purée to make the soup a vibrant green color. Heat to just below the boil. Season with salt and lemon juice. Garnish with the mussels and serve.

# Potlikker Soup

*My friend Angie Mosier, multitalented writer, cook, photographer, and food stylist, thinks of this soup as an ultimate winter comfort food. Traditionally the greens and potlikker would be served separately, but for this hearty soup the greens are cut smaller and combined with the potlikker. And, naturally, the soup should, be accompanied by hot cornbread.*

MAKES 8 SERVINGS

---

8 cups water or chicken or ham stock (page 23)

4 slices good-quality smoked bacon (I like Benton's, from Tennessee), chopped

1 medium onion, diced

2 garlic cloves, minced

1 teaspoon crushed red pepper flakes or 1 teaspoon seeded and minced jalapeño or Serrano pepper

3 pounds collard, turnip, or mustard greens, or a combination, washed, stemmed, and roughly torn or chopped into 2-inch-square pieces

1 tablespoon sugar

1 teaspoon salt

---

In a medium saucepan, bring the water or stock to a simmer and keep it hot but not boiling.

In a large stockpot, slowly cook the bacon until it's browned and the fat is rendered, about 8 minutes. Add the onions and cook over medium-high heat until they are soft and translucent but not brown, about 3 minutes. Add the garlic and stir with a wooden spoon for about 30 seconds, being careful not to let it brown. Add the pepper flakes or peppers and then add the greens in batches as the ones in the pot wilt and create room for more. Keep turning the greens, being careful not to let them stick to the bottom of the pan and brown. The greens will pop and sizzle as they release their liquid. Sprinkle in the sugar and continue turning the greens until they are all wilted and dark green.

Add the warm water to the pot, stir, and cover. Reduce the heat to low and simmer for 45 minutes to 1 hour. Add the salt.

## POTLIKKER

This much-loved green liquid, whose name is derived from the term "pot liquor," is simply the broth left over from cooking greens. It's valued not only for its flavor but also as a home remedy; some people even fancy it's an aphrodisiac. There's reason to believe it has medicinal uses: the vitamins and minerals that leach out of the greens in the cooking process remain in the potlikker. It can be drunk or even applied topically. The hunchback in Carson McCullers's *The Ballad of the Sad Café* "always smelled slightly of turnip greens, as Miss Amelia rubbed him night and morning with pot liquor to give him strength."

Potlikker entered the national consciousness during the Great Potlikker and Cornbread Debate of 1931. John T. Edge of the Southern Foodways Alliance wrote a master's thesis on this debate, in which Julian Harris, an editor of the *Atlanta Constitution*, took on Senator Huey Long of Louisiana over the proper way to eat cornbread and potlikker. Harris asserted that the cornbread must be crumbled. Long dunked his. This heated debate raged in newspapers and newsreels in February and March 1931 and ended without a definitive resolution. (I must confess, though, that members of my family are all crumblers.)

# Spicy Collard and Black-Eyed Pea Soup

*This spicy soup, with its promise of both good luck and money, is perfect for a New Year's Day lunch. The heat can be adjusted downward for those with timid palates (most of it comes from the chili and adobo), and it's possible to make a vegetarian version by substituting a couple of tablespoons of olive oil for the bacon and vegetable stock or water for the chicken or ham stock. I find, however, that the bacon gives the soup an appealing smokiness.*

MAKES 6 SERVINGS

2 slices thick-cut bacon, cut crosswise into
    half-inch-wide strips

2 medium onions, chopped

2 celery stalks, chopped

4 garlic cloves, minced

2 cups dried black-eyed peas

8 cups chicken stock or ham stock (page 23)
    (or canned low-sodium chicken broth)

1 pound collard greens, washed, stems removed,
    and chopped into 1-inch pieces

1 (16-ounce) can fire-roasted tomatoes

1 teaspoon ground cumin

1 teaspoon dried oregano

1 teaspoon hot sauce, or more to taste

1 chipotle chili from a can of chipotles in adobo,
    seeded and chopped

2 teaspoons adobo sauce

2 teaspoons salt

½ teaspoon freshly ground black pepper

In a large pot over medium heat, sauté the bacon until it begins to release its fat. Add the onions and celery and cook until the vegetables are beginning to brown. Add the garlic and cook until fragrant, about 30 seconds.

Add the black-eyed peas and 6 cups of the stock. Bring to a boil and simmer until the peas are tender, about 45 minutes.

Add the collards, the remaining stock, the tomatoes with their liquid, and the seasonings. Bring back to the boil and simmer for an additional 30 minutes. Taste for salt, adding more to taste.

Serve with cornbread, pepper vinegar, and additional hot sauce for the chili heads.

# Warm Turnip Greens Dip

*This southern riff on the hot artichoke dip that has seemed to be omnipresent at cocktail parties for decades is well worth a try. Most recipes for this dip call for frozen turnip greens, but, as a rule, fresh greens give a better flavor and texture. This is one instance, however, when you can use packaged, prewashed greens that still have the stems. The mixture is pulsed in the food processor, and the stems give a bit of added texture.*

MAKES 10–12 APPETIZER SERVINGS

5 slices bacon, cut crosswise into 1/4-inch-wide pieces

1/2 medium onion, chopped

2 garlic cloves, chopped

1 1/2 pounds turnip greens, washed and chopped into
    1-inch pieces

1/4 cup dry white wine

12 ounces cream cheese, cut into small pieces

8 ounces sour cream

1/2 teaspoon crushed red pepper flakes

1/4 teaspoon salt

3/4 cup freshly grated Parmesan cheese

Preheat oven to 350°. Butter a 6-cup oven-safe baking dish.

In a Dutch oven, cook the bacon over medium heat until crisp. Remove the bacon and all but about a tablespoon of the rendered bacon fat. Add the onions and cook over low heat until soft and translucent. Add the garlic and cook until fragrant, about 30 seconds. Add the turnip greens and the white wine. Cover and cook until the greens are wilted.

Remove the greens to a food processor and chop to a coarse purée. Add the cream cheese, sour cream, red pepper flakes, salt, and half the grated Parmesan. Pulse until the dip is thoroughly mixed, scraping the bowl as needed.

Turn the mixture into the prepared dish and top with the remaining Parmesan. Bake for 30 minutes and then turn the oven to broil to brown the top. You can also refrigerate the dip to cook it later. If it is refrigerated, cover the dish with aluminum foil and bake for half an hour at 350°, then remove the foil and bake for another half hour. Put it under the broiler for a few minutes at the end to brown the top.

Sprinkle the dip with the reserved bacon, and serve with crackers, pita chips, or—best of all—tortilla chips.

# Sides and Salads

It's hard to imagine a proper southern meal without a side of greens. Plenty of other cuisines use them as a side dish as well. You can perk up roasts or grilled meats by offering greens dishes with different seasonings and textures.

# Beans and Greens

*Mike and I often serve hot beans and greens as an accompaniment to grilled meats or cold ones as a part of a summer buffet. Substitute water or vegetable stock for the chicken stock, and serve over rice, and it becomes an easy vegetarian meal.*

MAKES 6 SERVINGS

---

2 tablespoons olive oil

1 small onion, sliced

2 garlic cloves, mashed

$\frac{1}{4}$ teaspoon crushed red pepper flakes

1 pound greens (kale, mustard greens, turnip greens, dandelion greens, beet greens, or a combination), washed, stemmed, and cut into $\frac{1}{2}$-inch pieces

1 (15$\frac{1}{2}$-ounce) can cannellini beans, drained and rinsed

1 cup chicken stock

2 tablespoons vinegar

Salt and freshly ground black pepper, to taste

Freshly grated Parmesan cheese, for garnish

---

In a large nonstick frying pan with a cover, sauté the onions in the olive oil until soft and translucent. Add the garlic and red pepper flakes and sauté for half a minute longer.

Add the greens and beans to the pan and stir to mix the vegetables together. Add the chicken stock, cover the pan, and cook until the greens are tender, about 10 minutes. Uncover the pan and stir until all the moisture has evaporated, raising the heat if necessary. Stir in the vinegar. Season with salt and pepper and sprinkle with Parmesan cheese before serving.

# Brazilian-Style Collards

*Collards* (couve à mineira) *are a traditional accompaniment to* feijoada, *the Brazilian national dish of black beans cooked with beef or pork parts. Being a southerner, I was always skeptical about any kind of cooking method for greens other than the traditional long, slow braising. This is the dish that changed my mind about quick-cooked greens. The secret of this dish, I think, is to cut the greens into a very thin chiffonade and not to be stingy with the seasonings. You may make this a vegetarian dish, albeit with a different flavor profile, by substituting olive oil for the bacon fat. Serve it as a side with almost any main dish.*

MAKES 8 SERVINGS

---

2 pounds collard greens, washed and stemmed

3 slices bacon, chopped

¼ cup finely chopped garlic (about 8–10 cloves)

¼ teaspoon crushed red pepper flakes

2 tablespoons fresh lemon juice

Salt and freshly ground black pepper, to taste

---

In batches, stack the collard leaves, roll them into a cigar shape, and cut them crosswise into a very thin chiffonade (no thicker than ⅛ inch).

In a Dutch oven, cook the bacon over medium heat until crisp. Add the garlic and red pepper flakes, and cook until you can smell the garlic, about 30 seconds. Add the greens and stir to coat with the bacon fat. Cook until the greens are tender, about five minutes, adding a little water if they stick to the bottom of the pan. They should be bright green and just tender. Toss with the lemon juice, season with salt and pepper, and serve at once.

# Collard Greens Gratin

*Baked in a cast-iron skillet, this delicious, cheesy collard green gratin, adapted from Fred Thompson and Belinda Ellis's* Edible Piedmont, *elevates the lowly collard green to the perfect accompaniment to an important dinner. It can stand up to duck, lamb, or grilled meats. We've also served it as a brunch dish, perfect alongside sausages or ham.*

MAKES 6 SERVINGS

4 ounces thinly sliced prosciutto or country ham
1 cup coarse unseasoned bread crumbs or panko
4 tablespoons olive oil, divided
1 teaspoon chopped fresh thyme
$\frac{1}{2}$ cup freshly grated Parmesan cheese, divided
Salt and freshly ground black pepper, to taste
1 pound collard greens, washed, stemmed,
    and roughly chopped
1 large onion, thinly sliced
2 garlic cloves, finely chopped
2 tablespoons unsalted butter
1 tablespoon all-purpose flour
1 cup whole milk
$\frac{1}{2}$ cup grated Gruyère
$\frac{1}{8}$ teaspoon freshly grated nutmeg

Preheat the oven to 325°. Place the ham on a baking sheet lined with parchment paper and bake until crisp, 20–25 minutes. Let cool and break into pieces. Turn up the oven temperature to 400°.

Combine the bread crumbs and 2 tablespoons of the olive oil in a medium skillet over medium heat; toast, tossing occasionally, until golden brown and crisp, 5–10 minutes. Remove from the heat and add the thyme and ¼ cup of the Parmesan. Season with salt and pepper. Stir in the ham and set aside.

Cook the collard greens in a large pot of boiling salted water until tender and bright green, about 5 minutes. Drain, transfer to a bowl of ice water, and let cool. Drain and squeeze dry with paper towels. Coarsely chop the greens and place in a large bowl.

Heat the remaining olive oil in a medium saucepan over medium heat. Add the onions and cook, stirring often, until softened and golden, 15–20 minutes. Stir in the garlic and cook until fragrant, about 30 seconds. Transfer the vegetables to the bowl with the greens and set aside.

Add the butter to the same saucepan and melt it over medium heat. Add the flour and cook, whisking constantly, until the mixture is smooth and very pale brown, about 4 minutes. Gradually whisk in the milk, a little at a time. Bring the mixture to a boil, reduce the heat, and add the Gruyère, stirring until the sauce is smooth and begins to thicken. Whisk in the remaining Parmesan and the nutmeg. Pour about half the sauce into the collard green mixture and stir to combine. Add enough sauce to bind the collards to a thick but not runny texture. Transfer the collard green mixture to a 10-inch cast-iron skillet, gratin dish, or pie plate. Top with the bread crumb mixture, place on a rimmed baking sheet, and bake until the gratin is bubbling, about 15–20 minutes. Let cool slightly before serving.

# Collard Greens and Brussels Sprouts with Gremolata

*Mike and I got the idea of combining collard greens and Brussels sprouts from Carla Hall's book* Cooking with Love. *She separates the sprouts into individual leaves, but we decided to substitute one of our favorite ways of cooking them, slicing the sprouts with the slicing blade of a food processor, then sautéing them in olive oil. Combine the greens and sprouts, then top them, as Carla does, with a lemon, parsley, and garlic gremolata.*

MAKES 8 SERVINGS

FOR THE GREMOLATA

Zest of 1 lemon
1 garlic clove, crushed with a garlic press
¼ cup chopped flat-leaf parsley
2 teaspoons olive oil
¼ cup freshly grated Parmesan cheese
Salt and freshly ground black pepper, to taste

FOR THE GREENS AND BRUSSELS SPROUTS

1 pound Brussels sprouts, sliced with the slicing blade of a
    food processor
5 tablespoons olive oil
Salt and freshly ground black pepper
2 pounds collard greens, washed, stemmed, and sliced into
    chiffonade
½ teaspoon salt
2 garlic cloves, peeled and left whole
1 teaspoon crushed red pepper flakes
¼ cup chicken stock, vegetable stock, or water

Make the gremolata by combining the lemon zest, garlic, parsley, olive oil, and Parmesan in a small bowl; season with salt and pepper and set aside.

Heat 2 tablespoons of the olive oil in a large frying pan. Add the Brussels sprouts and cook, stirring frequently, until they are tender and beginning to brown, about 5 minutes. Remove the sprouts from the pan, season with salt and pepper, and set aside.

In the same frying pan, heat the remaining olive oil; add the collard greens, in two batches if necessary, and stir until wilted, about 2 minutes. Add the salt, garlic, and red pepper flakes, stirring to blend, then add the stock or water. Bring to a boil, reduce the heat, and cook until the greens are tender and the liquid evaporates, about 10 minutes. Remove the garlic cloves and discard.

Stir the reserved Brussels sprouts into the greens, stir in the gremolata, reserving a portion to garnish the top, then check the seasoning, adding salt and pepper if needed. Serve immediately.

# Collards and Cornmeal Dumplings

*Mike and I developed this recipe to approximate the collards and cornmeal dumplings his grandmother made in coastal North Carolina. Cooking the collards in ham stock gives them a wonderful depth of flavor, but if you're pressed for time, you can still get good results by simply covering the greens with water and cooking them with a smoked ham hock. This ham stock (or the one on page 23), is handy to keep on hand. It can be frozen and used to add flavor to beans, soups, or any southern vegetable dish.*

MAKES 8 SERVINGS

---

FOR THE COLLARDS

1 onion, chopped

2 celery stalks, chopped

2 carrots, chopped

2 tablespoons bacon fat or olive oil

6 cups water

Ham bone and scraps from a baked ham, or 2 smoked ham hocks

1 bay leaf

$\frac{1}{2}$ teaspoon crushed red pepper flakes

Salt, to taste

3 pounds collard greens, washed, tough ribs removed, and cut into 2-inch pieces

FOR THE DUMPLINGS

1 cup white cornmeal

$\frac{1}{2}$ cup all-purpose flour

$\frac{1}{2}$ teaspoon salt

2 teaspoons baking powder

$1\frac{1}{2}$ tablespoons bacon grease, melted

$\frac{1}{2}$ cup milk

---

Sauté the onions, celery, and carrots in the bacon fat or olive oil until soft, about 15–20 minutes. Add the water and ham bone and scraps, bring to a boil, and simmer for 40–60 minutes. Strain the stock. Set the pork aside and when it's cool enough to handle, cut any remaining meat from the bone and chop into ¼-inch pieces.

Pour the stock into a large pot; add the red pepper flakes and bay leaf and season with salt. Bring to a boil and add the collards. (You might have to do this in batches, adding greens as the earlier batch wilts.) Cover and cook slowly until the greens are very tender, about 1½ hours. Add the pork.

During the last half hour that the greens are cooking, make the dumplings. In a mixing bowl, combine the cornmeal, flour, salt, and baking powder. Mix in the bacon grease and gradually add enough milk, to make a stiff batter (you may not need to use the entire ½ cup). Using your hands, form the batter into slightly flattened cakes about 1½ inches in diameter and ½ inch thick. Place the dumplings in a single layer on top of the cooked greens. Cover the pot and steam the dumplings until they puff and are soft to the touch, about 20 minutes.

To serve, place the dumplings in bowls with the collards on top and the broth ladled over all.

# Collards and Okra

*Southern home cooks frequently combine two or more of their favorite vegetables in a single dish—succotash; okra and tomatoes; okra and black-eyed peas; green beans and new potatoes. Collards and okra are also a great combination, and the crisp, bright-green okra pods are a useful corrective to those who think they don't like okra because it's slimy. If necessary, trim off the stem ends of the okra pods, which may be tough and hard.*

MAKES 8 SERVINGS

6 1/4-inch slices of salt pork, cut crosswise into
    1/4-inch lardoons
2 pounds collards, washed, stemmed, and cut into
    1-inch pieces
1/4 teaspoon crushed red pepper flakes, or more, to taste
3/4 cup water
16 whole pods of okra, stems removed

In a cast-iron or other heavy-bottomed pan, fry the salt pork over medium heat until the fat is rendered and the meat is starting to brown. Sprinkle in the red pepper and cook briefly. Add the collards and stir to coat them thoroughly with the fat. Add the water, cover, and cook over low heat until the greens are tender, about 40 minutes. Lay the okra over the top of the greens, cover again, and continue cooking until the okra is bright green and tender, about 10 minutes. Serve the okra pods on top of the collards.

# Creamed Collards

*A welcome change from the steakhouse classic creamed spinach, creamed collards have a slight bitterness that is mellowed by the richness of cream. Perhaps this isn't an everyday dish, but it's always a hit at holiday dinners. Add a couple of eggs, and the leftovers make a delicious quiche filling. Turnip greens or mustard greens can be substituted for the collards.*

MAKES 8 SERVINGS

---

2 tablespoons butter

½ medium onion, chopped

2 garlic cloves, thinly sliced

½ pound country ham, finely chopped

2 pounds collards, washed, stemmed, and cut into
    ½-inch strips

2 cups heavy cream

Salt and freshly ground black pepper, to taste

---

In a large frying pan, melt the butter over medium heat. Add the onions and garlic and sauté until the onions are soft and translucent, about 5 minutes, being careful not to let the garlic burn. Stir in the ham.

Add the collards in batches and toss until wilted. Pour in the cream, bring to a simmer, and cook until the collards are tender, the cream has reduced and thickened, and the mixture will mound in a spoon, about half an hour. Season with salt if needed (the ham will be salty), and freshly ground black pepper.

# Eastern North Carolina Collards

*The town of Ayden, North Carolina, calls itself the Collard Capital of the World, and its annual collard festival celebrates the leafy goodness of its favorite green vegetable with a beauty contest, a parade, and collard eating and cooking contests. The preferred collard in Ayden is the yellow cabbage collard, a local variety considered more tender and milder in flavor than garden-variety collards. Bum's Restaurant in downtown Ayden provides the collards for the festival's collard eating contest. Portions are neatly packed in pint-size Styrofoam containers, making it easy to calculate the weight of collards each contestant consumes (and keeps down for five minutes—one of the cardinal rules of the contest). Larry Dennis of Bum's boils his collards in one pot and in another makes "southern gravy," from pork parts and secret seasonings, then combines the two. Just a few minutes away at The Collard Shack, next door to the famed Skylight Inn barbecue restaurant, Vickie and Benny Cox specialize in yellow cabbage collards. You can buy the plants, the seeds, bags of collards, or cooked collards to take home.*

MAKES 8–10 SERVINGS

½ pound fresh pork (shoulder, tenderloin, or chops work just fine)

¼ pound slab bacon

¼ pound cured or country ham

4 pounds yellow cabbage collards (or ordinary collards if you can't find them, which you probably can't outside eastern North Carolina), washed, stemmed, and cut into 2-inch pieces

2 teaspoons crushed red pepper flakes

1 teaspoon Tabasco or other hot sauce

4 jalapeño peppers, seeded and chopped, for garnish

Put the meats in a large pot, cover with water, and bring to a boil. Reduce the heat and simmer for about an hour. Add the collards, red pepper, and Tabasco or other hot sauce and continue to simmer until the greens are very tender, about 2 hours longer.

Drain the greens in a colander, pressing out as much water as you can. Finely chop the meat and greens together. Serve garnished with the jalapeños.

Bum's serves collards with boiled potatoes and ham. If you want potatoes (I like fingerlings), add them to the pot about half an hour before the collards are done. Remove them before chopping the greens and meat.

# Eugene Walter's Sunday Greens

*The multitalented Eugene Walter (1921–98) is the author of* American Cooking: Southern Style *in the Time-Life Foods of the World
series. In* The Happy Table of Eugene Walter, *an unfinished cookbook edited by Donald Goodman, Walter's executor, and me and
published by UNC Press (2011), Walter distinguished between
Wednesday greens, which were for homefolks, and Sunday greens,
a somewhat fancier version for guests.*

MAKES 6 SERVINGS

4 slices fatback or bacon

1 medium onion, chopped

1 pound turnip greens, washed, stemmed, and chopped

Leaves from 1 bunch of radishes (optional)

1 smoked ham hock

½ teaspoon salt plus a pinch, divided

¼ teaspoon cayenne pepper

6 scallions, sliced

6 medium turnips

Pinch of sugar

2 tablespoons butter

2 tablespoons heavy cream

Pinch of freshly grated nutmeg or powdered mace

½ cup sippets (see Note)

In a large pot, fry the fatback or bacon over medium heat until the fat is rendered and the meat is cooked but not crisp. Sauté the onions in the fat until they are lightly browned.

Add the turnip greens, radish leaves, if using, ham hock, salt, cayenne pepper, scallions, and enough water almost to cover them. Bring to a boil and simmer over low heat, stirring occasionally, until the greens are tender, about 45 minutes (or "forever," as Walter directs).

Meanwhile, boil the turnips in a large pot of water with the remaining salt and the sugar just until they are fork-tender; drain, peel, and cube them. Return them to the pot and combine them with the butter, cream, and nutmeg or mace. Serve alongside the greens.

Turn the greens into a serving bowl with enough of the potlikker to cover them. Top with sippets.

NOTE ❋ "In North Alabama," Walter explains, "greens are often served with a good handful of sippets over them. These cubes of stale bread fried in bacon fat with a couple of unpeeled garlic toes in the skillet with them are usually known by their French name of croutons, but the ancient English name is sippets. Very fine they are with any dish of greens or any clear soup."

# Dandelion Greens with Garlic and Anchovies

*Those of us who live in herbicide- and pollution-ridden cities don't dare to pick dandelion greens, but they do make an appearance in the market occasionally. This quick Italian-style sauté of dandelion greens with pancetta, anchovy, and garlic can also be made with other tender greens. We use it as a side dish with grilled meats or as a flavorful bruschetta topping.*

MAKES 4 SERVINGS

1 tablespoon olive oil
1 ounce pancetta, finely chopped
2 anchovy fillets, chopped
½ small onion, finely chopped
2 garlic cloves, thinly sliced
¼ teaspoon red pepper flakes
2 bunches dandelion greens, washed, tough stems trimmed, and cut into 1-inch pieces
Juice of half a lemon

In a medium frying pan, cook the pancetta in the olive oil over medium heat until the pancetta renders its fat, about 3 minutes. Reduce the heat, add the anchovies, and cook until they are almost dissolved, about 2 minutes. Add the onions, garlic, and red pepper and sauté until the onion is soft and translucent, being careful not to burn the garlic.

Raise the heat to medium-high and add the chopped dandelion greens, tossing them in the fat until they are wilted. Sprinkle the lemon juice over the greens and serve immediately or spoon on grilled Italian bread slices as a bruschetta topping.

# Greens with Anchoïade

*A Provençal dish,* anchoïade *is a highly flavored mixture of garlic and anchovies that is often baked as a filling in bread or spread on bread as an appetizer. There are as many versions as there are Provençal cooks. This one works particularly well as a topping for a crouton in a bowl of greens and potlikker. For a more substantial luncheon or supper dish, top each serving with a poached egg.*

MAKES 4 SERVINGS

¼ cup olive oil
6 anchovy fillets, rinsed to remove some of the salt,
    and chopped
3 garlic cloves, finely chopped
1 medium tomato, peeled, seeded, and chopped
½ teaspoon freshly ground black pepper
8–10 basil leaves, chopped
4 (1-inch-thick) slices hearty Italian bread
1 recipe Basic Southern Greens and their potlikker (page 18)

Heat the oil in a small frying pan over low heat and cook the anchovies until they dissolve, about 3–4 minutes. Add the garlic and cook briefly, for about 30 seconds. Add the tomato and simmer until almost all the liquid has evaporated. Stir in the pepper and basil. Set aside.

Toast the bread slices and spread each with a quarter of the *anchoïade* mixture. Place each piece of bread in a soup plate, top with the greens, and moisten with about half a cup of potlikker.

# Kashmiri Greens

*Greens with chilies and asafetida is an everyday dish in Kashmir, and there are as many recipes for it as there are home cooks. The dish is good served simply on top of rice, but it makes a great side dish for an Indian meal. In Kashmir, it is made with various kinds of greens (the Kashmiri word* haak *simply means "greens."), so make it with whatever looks best in the market. Asafetida, which is available at Indian markets, is a powdered gum with a strong onion-garlic flavor. It should be used sparingly. Mustard oil can be found in specialty shops or ordered online.*

### MAKES 8 SERVINGS

½ cup mustard oil
¼ teaspoon asafetida
3 small dried hot red chilies
1 small onion, thinly sliced
1 tablespoon grated fresh ginger
2 garlic cloves, thinly sliced
1 teaspoon ground cumin
2 pounds greens (collards, mustard greens, turnip greens, beet greens, or kale), washed, dried, stemmed, and coarsely chopped
1 cup water
Salt and freshly ground black pepper, to taste
Cooked rice

Heat the oil over medium heat in a Dutch oven and add the asafetida and chilies. When the spices become fragrant, add the onions and cook until soft and translucent. Stir in the ginger, garlic, and cumin and cook until fragrant, about a minute.

Add the greens and stir to coat with the oil. Add the water, cover, and cook, stirring occasionally, until the greens are just tender, 15–20 minutes. Remove the chilies before serving and season with salt and pepper. Serve with the rice.

# Mixed Greens

*Southern cooks, depending on what was available in the market or garden, often mixed different kinds of greens together to make a mess of greens for dinner. My cousin Daisy McBride Johnson, a gifted cook from Harrisonburg, Louisiana, printed a handwritten collection of her recipes for her children and grandchildren. As her mother taught her, she always cooked turnip greens and mustard greens together, and this is the way her daughter, Emmilee Green, who now lives in the family home, cooks them today. They were always accompanied by "good pepper sauce" and cornbread. This recipe is based on her method.*

### MAKES 8 SERVINGS

½ pound salt pork

1 pound turnip greens, "which have been washed and
  washed thoroughly," as Daisy put it, stemmed,
  and cut into 1-inch pieces

1 pound mustard greens, washed, stemmed, and cut into
  1-inch pieces

½ teaspoon crushed red pepper flakes

2 garlic cloves, peeled and left whole

Cover the pork with water in a Dutch oven. Bring to a boil, reduce the heat, and simmer until the pork is tender when tested with a fork, about 30 minutes.

Remove the pork from the pan and reserve; add the greens, and cook over low heat until tender, about 45 minutes.

Cut the pork into serving-size pieces and serve with the greens.

# Mustard Greens Punjabi-Style
## (Sarson Da Saag)

*Every household in the Punjab region of India makes a different version of* sarson da saag. *This version, adapted from Madhur Jaffrey's* World-of-the-East Vegetarian Cooking, *combines two southern American staples, mustard greens and cornmeal but flavors them in an unexpected way—with ginger, garlic, and chilies. The greens are traditionally served with* makki roti, *a cornmeal flatbread, but good old southern cornpone works almost as well. It's an excellent, if untraditional, accompaniment for any grilled meat.*

MAKES 8 SERVINGS

2 pounds mustard greens, washed, stemmed,
   and roughly chopped

1 pound spinach, washed and roughly chopped

3 tablespoons olive oil

½ onion, chopped

1 fresh hot green chili pepper, such as a jalapeño or Serrano,
   stemmed, seeded, and chopped

2 garlic cloves, minced

2 tablespoons grated fresh ginger

½ cup unsalted butter

5 tablespoons cornmeal

2 teaspoons salt

Bring 2 cups of water to a boil in a large pot. Add the mustard greens and spinach and cook, uncovered, until the greens are wilted and tender, about 10–15 minutes.

Meanwhile, heat the olive oil in a frying pan over medium heat and cook the onion until translucent. Add the chili peppers, garlic, and ginger root and sauté until fragrant, about 30 seconds. Remove from heat.

Drain the greens and add them, along with the onion-garlic mixture, to the container of a food processor or heavy-duty blender. Process into a rough purée.

In the same frying pan you used to cook the onions, melt the butter and add the cornmeal. Cook for about 2 minutes, stirring constantly, lowering the heat if needed to keep the cornmeal from browning. Add the greens, salt, and enough water to thin out the mixture. Cook over low heat for about 10 minutes to blend flavors.

# Mustard Greens Salad

*This version of the traditional southern wilted lettuce salad uses spicy mustard greens instead and substitutes olive oil for the usual bacon fat. If you're watching calories, you can use less oil without seriously affecting the flavor. The assertive flavors of this salad make it a good accompaniment to grilled meats as part of a summer meal.*

MAKES 8 SERVINGS

½ pound mustard greens
4½ teaspoons light brown sugar
⅛ cup apple cider vinegar
½ teaspoon Worcestershire sauce
3 tablespoons extra-virgin olive oil
¼ teaspoon salt
¼ teaspoon freshly ground black pepper

Wash the greens well and drain or spin them dry in a salad spinner. Remove the tough stems, chop into 1-inch pieces, and place in a large bowl.

Combine the remaining ingredients in a small saucepan and heat just until boiling. Pour the hot dressing over the greens, toss to combine, and serve immediately.

# Mustard Greens with Chipotle Chiles and Chorizo

*Chipotles are simply smoked jalapeño peppers, available dried in Latin markets and canned in adobo sauce in most supermarkets. Their heat and smoky earthiness seem to have a special affinity for greens, but be sure to use them sparingly, at least at first. One, or at most two, canned chipotles should give sufficient heat for a pot of greens. You can store the unused chipotles for a week or two in the refrigerator, but for longer storage, freeze them in small quantities for later use.*

MAKES 6 SERVINGS

---

2 links Mexican-style chorizo, cut into 1-inch pieces

½ white onion, diced

1½ pounds mustard greens, washed, stemmed, and cut into 1-inch squares

1 canned chipotle, finely chopped, with 2 teaspoons adobo sauce from the can

6 cups homemade chicken or ham stock or reduced-sodium commercial chicken stock

Salt, to taste

---

In a large casserole with a lid, cook the chorizo over medium heat, crumbling it with a wooden spoon until it is beginning to brown. Remove the chorizo from the pan with a slotted spoon and set aside. Add the onions to the fat remaining in the pan (you may need to add a tablespoon or so of olive oil if there isn't enough fat), and cook until soft and translucent.

Add the greens, tossing until wilted and coated with the fat. Add the chicken or ham stock and the chipotle. Cover and cook until the greens are tender, about 40 minutes. Serve garnished with the crumbled chorizo.

# Oysters Rockefeller with Collards

*Oysters Rockefeller originated at Antoine's in New Orleans and remains the venerable restaurant's most famous dish. Using collards instead of spinach puts a hearty, full-flavored country spin on this fancy Creole favorite. Use the youngest collards you can find—baby collards if possible. We often serve these with cocktails, but they work equally well as a first course.*

MAKES 4 APPETIZER SERVINGS

1 dozen oysters on the half shell

Rock salt, for the baking pan

4 tablespoons butter

4 scallions, chopped

2 garlic cloves, minced

¼ pound country ham, finely chopped

½ cup dry white wine

4 cups, washed, stemmed, and coarsely chopped collards

⅓ cup heavy cream

1 dash Tabasco or other hot sauce

Salt and freshly ground black pepper, if needed

½ cup bread crumbs

¼ cup finely chopped parsley

⅓ cup freshly grated Parmesan cheese

Preheat the oven to 450°.

Pour a layer of rock salt (enough to keep the oysters level) into a baking pan and place the oysters on top; set aside.

Melt the butter in a frying pan and sauté the scallions until tender. Add the ham and garlic and cook just until the garlic is aromatic but not brown. Add the white wine, then stir in the collards. Cover and cook on low heat until the greens are wilted, about 5 minutes. Uncover, raise the heat, and continue cooking until most of the moisture has evaporated. Purée the collard mixture in a food processor. Stir in the cream. Add the Tabasco and season with salt and pepper.

Mix together the bread crumbs, parsley, and Parmesan in a small bowl.

Place about a tablespoon of the collard purée on top of each oyster, then sprinkle with the bread crumb mixture.

Bake until the bread crumbs and cheese are brown, about 8 minutes. Serve immediately.

# Spicy Collard Greens in Tomato Sauce

*In my family, we ate mostly turnip greens and occasionally mustard greens, never collards. The same seems to have been true in the part of Virginia where chef Edna Lewis grew up. Scott Peacock, the coauthor of Lewis's final book,* The Gift of Southern Cooking, *relates that Miss Lewis "maintains a prejudice against" collards, except when cooked with tomatoes. This recipe is inspired by her preference.*

MAKES 8 SERVINGS

---

1 quart Ham Stock (page 23)
¼ cup bacon fat
1 medium onion, coarsely chopped
4 garlic cloves, minced
1 teaspoon crushed red pepper flakes
Salt and freshly ground black pepper, to taste
2 pounds collard greens, washed, stemmed, and cut into
    1-inch-wide ribbons
1 (28-ounce) can whole peeled tomatoes with their juice

---

In a medium Dutch oven heat the bacon fat over medium heat; add the oil and onions and cook until the onions are soft and translucent, about 5 minutes. Add the garlic and red pepper and season with salt and pepper. Cook for about 30 seconds more.

Add the ham stock. Bring to a boil and add the collards, in batches if necessary. Simmer until the greens are tender, about 40 minutes. Break up the tomatoes by squeezing them in your hands and add them and their liquid and simmer for another 15 minutes to blend the flavors.

# Sweet Corn and Turnip Greens

*This recipe, a delicious combination of the slight bitterness of turnip greens and the sweetness of summer corn, is based on a recipe from Gary Gee's blog* The Kitchen *(www.mycookingblog.com). It's worth cooking up a batch of turnip greens for and is also a great way to use up leftover greens. If fresh corn is not in season, frozen can be substituted.*

### MAKES 8 SERVINGS

1 recipe Basic Southern Greens (page 18), made with
  turnip greens
3 cups sweet corn, cut off the cob, or frozen sweet corn,
  thawed
2 medium tomatoes, seeded and chopped
Crushed red pepper flakes, to taste
1 tablespoon vinegar (optional)
Salt and freshly ground black pepper, to taste

Bring the greens to a boil. Add the corn and return to the boil. Add the tomatoes, red pepper, and vinegar (if you haven't already added it to the basic recipe). Cook until the corn is warmed through. Season with salt and pepper.

# Vegetarian Slow-Cooker Collard Greens

*The traditional way of cooking southern greens is with smoked pork, but it's possible to make a vegetarian version and still have a bit of smoky flavor by seasoning them with smoked paprika. The slow cooker makes preparation a breeze, and the timing is not critical. (You can also make a nonvegetarian version by sautéing the onion in bacon fat and adding a ham hock when the greens begin to cook.)*

MAKES 8 SERVINGS

---

2 tablespoons olive oil
1 large onion, chopped
6 garlic cloves, sliced
2 cups vegetable stock or water
¼ cup apple cider vinegar
1 tablespoon smoked paprika
1 teaspoon crushed red pepper flakes
2 pounds collard greens, washed, stemmed,
   and chopped into 2-inch pieces
Salt and freshly ground black pepper, to taste

---

Heat the olive oil in a large frying pan or Dutch oven over medium heat. Add the onion and sauté until soft and translucent. Add the garlic and cook until it is fragrant, about 30 seconds. Add the stock or water, vinegar, paprika, and red pepper and bring to a boil.

Pour the liquid into a slow cooker. Add the greens and stir to moisten. Cover and cook on low for about 4 hours. Season with salt and pepper.

# Wilted Lettuce Salad

*These days it's possible to buy leaf lettuce in almost any grocery store, but when I was growing up in North Louisiana, the only lettuce available in the grocery store was iceberg. This salad was a springtime treat, available only in the couple of weeks between the time the lettuce came up and the time the weather became too hot, the lettuce bolted, and the leaves became bitter.*

MAKES 4 SERVINGS

6 slices bacon

8 cups Boston or other tender leaf lettuce, washed, dried, and torn into bite-size pieces

6 green onions with tops, thinly sliced

$\frac{1}{4}$ cup apple cider vinegar

2 tablespoons water

1 tablespoon sugar

$\frac{1}{2}$ teaspoon freshly ground black pepper

1 hard-boiled egg, roughly chopped

Fry the bacon over medium heat until very crisp. Remove the bacon from the pan, leaving the bacon grease in the skillet. Put the greens and green onions into a large salad bowl and crumble the bacon over the top.

To the hot bacon drippings in the frying pan add the vinegar, water, sugar, and pepper. Stir over medium heat until heated through.

Pour the hot salad dressing over the greens and toss thoroughly. Garnish with chopped hard-boiled egg. Serve immediately.

# Main Courses

Greens, traditionally a side dish in the South, can also come front and center as main courses. Bake them in a tart, serve them atop grits or polenta, even make them into a sandwich.

# Collard, Ham, and Potato Cobbler with Cornbread Crust

*We love to make chicken pie with a cornbread topping rather than the conventional piecrust. This collard green and ham pie is a variation on the chicken pie. Combining three of the South's favorite ingredients, it might be even better than the original. It makes for a satisfying one-dish meal.*

MAKES 8 SERVINGS

### FOR THE FILLING

4 quarts water

1 ham hock

2 pounds collards, washed, stemmed, and cut into 1-inch pieces

1 pound Yukon Gold potatoes, peeled and cut into ½-inch cubes

4 slices bacon, cut into ¼-inch lardoons

2 medium onions, thinly sliced

4 garlic cloves, minced

1 teaspoon salt

1 teaspoon freshly ground black pepper

⅛ teaspoon crushed red pepper flakes

2 tablespoons all-purpose flour

1 cup country ham, chopped, or leftover baked ham, cut into ½-inch cubes

### FOR THE TOPPING

¾ cup yellow cornmeal

¼ cup all-purpose flour

¾ teaspoon salt

½ teaspoon baking powder

½ teaspoon baking soda

¾ cup buttermilk

1 large egg

1 tablespoon bacon fat

To make the filling, bring the water to a boil in a large stockpot; add the ham hock and simmer for half an hour. Add the collards, and cook until tender, about 40 minutes. In the last 10 minutes of the cooking time, add the potatoes. Drain the collards and potatoes, reserving the potlikker.

In a heavy pot, cook the bacon over medium heat until it is crisp and the fat is rendered. Remove the bacon, leaving the fat behind, and drain it on paper towels; set aside.

Cook the onion in the bacon fat until soft and translucent, about 10 minutes; add the garlic and cook until fragrant, about 30 seconds. Add the salt, pepper, and red pepper flakes. Cook on low heat for about 10 minutes for the flavors to blend. Stir in the flour and continue cooking until the flour is a light brown color, about 5 minutes longer. Add two cups of the reserved potlikker and stir to blend.

Add the ham, collards, and potatoes. Add a bit more of the potlikker, if needed, to make the mixture the consistency of a thin stew. Bring to a boil again, correct the seasonings, and remove from the heat. Pour the filling into a greased 10-inch cast iron skillet or baking dish.

To make the topping, preheat the oven to 350°.

In medium bowl, whisk together the cornmeal, flour, salt, baking powder, and baking soda. Measure the buttermilk in a 2-cup measuring cup, add the egg, and whisk until well blended. Add the wet ingredients to the dry and stir to combine; pour the cornbread mixture on top of the ham and collard filling, spreading it to the sides of the skillet.

Bake until the cornbread is brown on top and the filling is bubbling, about 25 minutes. Let stand for about 10 minutes before serving.

# Collard Greens Dolmas

*The rector of my church, the Reverend Kym Lucas, and her husband, Mark Retherford, have achieved something that many parents only dream of—they have instilled in each of their four children a love of greens. This recipe from Mark uses collard greens rather than the traditional grape leaves and is one of the children's favorite ways to eat collards.*

MAKES 8 SERVINGS

20 whole collard green leaves, washed
2 tablespoons olive oil
1 medium onion, finely chopped
2 garlic cloves, minced
½ pound ground lamb
1 teaspoon ground cinnamon
1 teaspoon ground cumin
1 cup cooked rice
½ cup chopped cherry tomatoes, chopped
¼ cup raisins
¼ cup pine nuts, toasted
Salt and freshly ground black pepper, to taste
¼ cup fresh lemon juice
⅔ cup water or chicken stock
Plain yogurt

Bring a large pot of water to a boil, add the collard greens, and cook briefly, about 5 minutes. Drain and dry them with paper towels, then lay each leaf on a flat surface and remove the center stem with a knife, leaving two half leaves.

Heat the oil in a large frying pan over medium heat and cook the onions and garlic until the onions are soft and translucent, about 5 minutes. Add the lamb and cook, stirring and breaking up the clumps, until the red color is gone, about 5 minutes more. If necessary, drain off any excess fat.

Add the cinnamon, cumin, rice, tomatoes, raisins, and pine nuts and season with salt and pepper.

Place about two teaspoonful of filling on the rib side of each half collard leaf, a third of the way from the top. Roll the top down over the filling and turn the sides toward the center, and continue rolling to make a cylindrical packet. Repeat with all the leaves.

Place the rolled dolmas in a single layer, seam side down, in a large frying pan or casserole with a cover. Sprinkle the lemon juice over the top. Add the water or stock and bring to a boil. (It helps to put a plate on top of the dolmas to keep them from unwinding.) Reduce the heat to low, cover the pan, and steam the dolmas gently until the greens are tender and the filling is hot, about 30 minutes.

Serve with yogurt.

# Collard Sandwich

*The collard sandwich seems to be a North Carolina specialty, and particularly for members of the Lumbee tribe, who live in and around Robeson County. It's a brilliant idea—collard greens and a couple of slices of fried fatback between two pieces of fried cornbread. You can eat these sandwiches at the Lumbee Homecoming held every year in Pembroke, North Carolina, during the week of July 4, but they are most often found at fairs and festivals, UPro, a restaurant in Aberdeen, North Carolina, claims to be "home of the collard green sandwich" and serves them every day. Fried cornbread sometimes goes by the name "hoecake," which has come to mean a softer, leavened cake, sometimes made with a combination of cornmeal and flour. I think a firmer batter, like the one for what I call hot-water cornbread, yields a cake that is closer in spirit to the original hoecake, which was cooked on a griddle called a "hoe," and works better for this sandwich. The sandwich is a great way to use leftover collards.*

### MAKES 4 SERVINGS

---

8 slices fatback (or "streak o' lean"), sliced about ⅜ inch thick
½ recipe Basic Southern Greens (page 18), made with
  collards and fatback instead of bacon and including all the
  options—onion, garlic, red pepper flakes, and vinegar
1 recipe Hot-Water Cornbread (recipe follows)
Pepper vinegar (optional)

---

Prepare the collards for cooking as indicated in the recipe. In a large Dutch oven, fry the fatback over medium heat until the fat has been rendered and the meat is crisp. Set the meat aside. Use the fat remaining in the pan to cook the collard greens according to the directions in the recipe. To assemble the sandwiches, drain the collards. (You want them to be fairly dry so that the potlikker won't cause the corn cakes to disintegrate.) Pile about half a cup of collards on top of each of four corncakes and sprinkle with pepper vinegar, if using, top with two slices of the fried fatback and then another corncake.

# Hot-Water Cornbread

*My mother loved hot-water cornbread, which we often had with greens and other southern vegetables, and it has become a part of the family repertoire. It's a very simple cornbread preparation, and exact measurements aren't as important as the desired consistency of the batter, which varies dramatically from cook to cook. It is sometimes made with a thinner batter that is dropped into the hot oil from a spoon, almost like a pancake batter. This recipe calls for a rather stiff batter. Mike sometimes makes quarter-size cornbread croutons to float in soup. We usually just use vegetable oil for frying, but it's even better if you have bacon fat.*

MAKES 8 (4- TO 5-INCH) CAKES

---

2 cups yellow cornmeal
1½ teaspoons salt
1–2 cups boiling water
Vegetable oil or bacon fat for frying

---

In a medium-size bowl, combine the cornmeal and salt. Add enough of the water to produce a firm dough that holds together when pressed with your hands. Form the dough by tablespoonful into flat disks 4–5 inches in diameter.

Preheat the oven to 200°.

Heat about ¼ inch of vegetable oil or bacon fat in a cast-iron skillet. Working in batches, cook the disks until brown around the edges. Flip and brown the other side. Keep warm in the oven while frying the rest of the corn cakes. Serve hot.

# Braised Pork Shoulder with Greens and Grits

*Greens occupy a prominent place in New Orleans chef Alex Harrell's cooking. After four years at the southern gastropub Sylvain, Harrell left to start his own restaurant, Angeline, which opened in March 2015. At Sylvain, this braised pork shoulder was a signature dish for the Alabama-born chef. At first reading this looks like a complicated recipe for the home cook, but the pork shoulder can be cooked in advance and refrigerated, or even frozen. The greens can be cooked earlier in the day and reheated. Thanks to Chef Harrell for sharing the recipe.*

## MAKES 8 SERVINGS

### FOR THE PORK SHOULDER

4 pounds pork shoulder, cut into 2-pound pieces

1 uncured pork hock

½ cup white wine

2 bay leaves

6 sprigs plus 1 tablespoon chopped fresh thyme, divided

3 garlic cloves

1 onion, roughly chopped

2 celery stalks, roughly chopped

1 carrot, roughly chopped

2 sprigs rosemary

½ cup Dijon mustard

2 tablespoons chopped chives

1 tablespoon chopped parsley

½ teaspoon chili powder

Salt and freshly ground black pepper, to taste

3 slices bacon, diced

$1/2$ medium onion, cut into medium dice

1 tablespoon chopped garlic

$1/2$ cup apple cider vinegar

$3/8$ cup brown sugar

$1/2$ pounds greens (collards, mustard greens, or turnip greens), washed, stemmed, and cut into 1-inch pieces

2 cups homemade or commercial low-sodium chicken stock

1 cup water

$1/2$ teaspoons hot sauce

2 tablespoons Worcestershire sauce

Salt and freshly ground black pepper, to taste

FOR THE GRITS

1 cup milk

1 cup water

2 cups heavy cream

Salt and freshly ground black pepper, to taste

1 cup stone-ground grits

FOR FINAL PREPARATION

3 tablespoons olive oil

---

Put the pork shoulder, pork hock, wine, bay leaves, thyme sprigs, garlic, onions, celery, carrots, and rosemary into a deep stock-pot. Cover with cold water by 2 inches. Bring to a boil, then reduce heat to a simmer and cook until the meat is tender, about 3 hours. Remove the meat and allow to cool.

Strain the cooking liquid and skim away any fat. Wipe the stockpot clean, return the cooking liquid to the pot, and boil until reduced by half. Set aside.

When the meat is cool enough to handle, pick over the meat and hock, removing all the fat, skin, bones, and sinew. Chop the meat coarsely. In a large bowl, combine the meat with the remaining thyme and the mustard, chives, parsley, and chili powder and season with salt and pepper. With a wooden spoon, beat in about ¾ cup of the reduced cooking liquid to moisten the mixture. Form the meat mixture into a log shape about 3 inches in diameter. Wrap the log in plastic wrap and refrigerate for at least 4 hours and up to 3 days.

To prepare the greens, in a medium Dutch oven, cook the bacon over medium heat until crisp. Remove the bacon, leaving the fat behind, and set aside. Add the onions and garlic and sauté for about 10 minutes. Add the vinegar and brown sugar and cook for 5 minutes. Add the greens and toss until wilted. Add the bacon, stock, water, hot sauce, and Worcestershire sauce, season with salt and pepper, and simmer until the greens are tender, about 40 minutes.

To make the grits, combine the milk, water, and cream in a medium saucepan and bring to a simmer over medium heat. Season with salt and pepper. Whisk in the grits and continue to stir until the liquid returns to a simmer and the grits begin to thicken. Reduce the heat and cook slowly, about 20 minutes. Adjust the seasonings to taste.

Slice the pork roll into roughly 1-inch-thick rounds. Heat the olive oil in a frying pan over medium heat and sear the pork rounds until they are heated through; they should be brown and crusty on the outside but still creamy on the inside.

To serve, in the center of each serving plate, put a layer of grits, a layer of greens, and top with 2 rounds of the pork roll.

# Gumbo z'Herbes

*This hearty gumbo of greens and meats is traditionally eaten in New Orleans on Holy Thursday before fasting on Good Friday. New Orleans's authority on Gumbo z'Herbes is Leah Chase, who serves it at her New Orleans restaurant Dooky Chase every Holy Thursday. Chase's version, which uses 9 kinds of greens and a variety of meats, is not vegetarian, but vegetarian gumbos are often served in Louisiana during the period of Lenten fasting. What is important, she says, is to use an odd number of greens. The number of different greens used determines the number of friends you will make in the coming year.*

### MAKES 8–10 SERVINGS

3 pounds greens (a combination of mustard greens, collards, turnip greens, beet greens, radish leaves, watercress, kale, parsley, and/or others), washed, tough stems removed, and chopped into 1-inch pieces

½ cup vegetable oil

½ cup all-purpose flour

2 cups, finely chopped onions

1 cup finely chopped green bell peppers

1 cup finely chopped red bell peppers

1 cup finely chopped celery

6 garlic cloves, finely chopped

2 teaspoons cayenne pepper

Water, ham stock (page 23), or chicken stock

1 ham hock or 1 pound smoked sausage (optional)

Cooked rice

Scallion tops, coarsely chopped, for garnish

Parsley, coarsely chopped, for garnish

In a large pot, cover the greens with water and bring to a boil over high heat. Reduce the heat to a simmer and cook the greens until tender, about 40 minutes. Drain the greens, reserving the liquid.

Meanwhile, make a roux: In a heavy-bottomed pot, heat the vegetable oil and whisk in the flour. Cook over low heat, stirring constantly, until the flour is a light brown color, about 10 minutes. Add the onions, bell peppers, celery, garlic, and cayenne and continue to cook over low heat until the vegetables are tender.

Transfer the vegetables to the pot the greens were cooked in. Measure the reserved cooking liquid and add enough water, ham stock, or chicken stock to make 2 quarts. Add the liquid to the pot. Add the ham hock or smoked sausage, if using. Simmer for about an hour.

Skim the fat off the top if necessary. Serve with the rice and garnish with the scallions and parsley.

# Mustard Greens and Andouille Tart with Cornmeal Crust

*This hearty tart makes a good brunch or supper dish. I like the spiciness of mustard greens, but you can substitute any other greens you have on hand. The restrained heat of the andouille sausage seems perfect in this tart, but if you can't find it, spicy Italian sausage will work just fine. The cornmeal crust cooks up crisp, and the dough is very easy to work.*

MAKES 8 SERVINGS

FOR THE CRUST

1¼ cups all-purpose flour, plus more for the work surface
¾ cup yellow or white stone-ground cornmeal
¾ teaspoon salt
½ cup unsalted butter, chilled and cut into small pieces
1 large egg yolk
3–6 tablespoons ice water

FOR THE FILLING

6 ounces andouille sausage, skinned and roughly chopped
½ medium onion, chopped
1 garlic clove, minced
1 pound mustard greens, washed, tough stems removed, and chopped
¼ cup water
1 cup milk
2 large eggs
¼ teaspoon salt
A few grinds of black pepper
1 cup grated Gruyère

To make the crust, put the flour, cornmeal, and salt into the bowl of a food processor and pulse to mix. Add the butter and pulse a few times until it is roughly incorporated. Whisk the egg yolk with 3 tablespoons of the water, and with the machine running, pour the mixture in slowly until the dough just comes together. If the dough seems too crumbly, add another 1–2 tablespoons of water and continue processing until it gathers into a ball. Wrap the dough in plastic wrap and refrigerate for an hour or overnight.

Preheat the oven to 350°.

Roll out the crust to a 10-inch circle and press it into a 9-inch tart pan with a removable bottom.

Prick the bottom of the shell thoroughly with a fork. Cover it with a piece of crumpled parchment paper, fill it with pie weights (or rice or beans), and bake for 20 minutes. Remove the paper and weights and continue baking for another 10 minutes, or until the crust is lightly brown and begins to pull away from the sides of the pan. Cool on a rack.

To make the filling, in a large pot over medium heat, sauté the sausage until it is cooked through and releases its fat. Remove the sausage, leaving the fat behind, and set aside. Add the onions and cook until they are soft and translucent, being careful not to brown them. Add the garlic and cook until fragrant, about 30 seconds. Add the greens and the water. Cover the pan and cook until the greens are wilted. Remove the lid and continue cooking until the remaining liquid evaporates. Remove from heat, and return the sausage to the pan, mixing well.

Beat together the milk, eggs, salt, and pepper.

Sprinkle half the cheese into the tart shell, then spoon in the filling, spreading it evenly to the edges. Pour in the milk and egg mixture and top with the rest of the cheese. Place the tart pan on a baking sheet and bake for about 40 minutes, or until the top is lightly brown and a knife inserted in the center comes out clean. (I like to put it under the broiler briefly at the end to make the top beautifully brown.) Remove to a rack.

Serve warm or at room temperature.

# Penne with Sausage and Collard Greens

*This simple pasta recipe is one of our regulars for an easy week-night supper. It's easy to prepare and can be used as a template for concocting a quick and easy supper out of whatever greens, sausage, and pasta you may have on hand. I'm especially fond of collards with pasta — they have more character than the usual kale.*

MAKES 4 SERVINGS

1 pound sweet Italian sausage

1 pound penne pasta

1 pound collard greens, washed, stemmed, and cut into
    1-inch slices

2 tablespoons olive oil, or more as needed

4 garlic cloves, finely chopped

½ teaspoon crushed red pepper flakes

Salt and freshly ground black pepper, to taste

¼ cup freshly grated Parmesan cheese, plus more for serving

Remove the sausage from the casings and cook it in a large frying pan over medium heat, breaking it up with a spatula, until no pink remains and the sausage begins to brown. Remove the sausage and set aside, leaving behind the fat.

Bring a large saucepan of water to a boil and salt generously; add the pasta and cook until it is al dente, about 8–10 minutes. Drain the pasta, reserving one cup of the cooking water.

Cook the garlic briefly in the sausage fat, about 30 seconds, then add the collards, olive oil, and red pepper flakes, season with salt and pepper, and stir to coat the collards with the fat. (You may need an additional tablespoon or two of olive oil, depending on how much fat the sausage has rendered.) Cover the pan and cook the collards until tender, about 10 minutes, adding half a cup of water, plus more if needed, to steam the collards.

Add the sausage and pasta to the collards, mixing thoroughly. Add the reserved pasta water, if needed, to moisten the dish. Cook for about 3 minutes to warm the dish through. Stir in the Parmesan.

Serve with additional Parmesan.

# Roast Chicken with Collard and Cornbread Stuffing

*Greens make a tasty and unusual addition to southern cornbread stuffing. If you are lucky enough to find baby collards at a farmers' market or specialty food store, you can use them in this recipe without stemming or precooking them.*

MAKES 6–8 SERVINGS

1 (4- to 6-pound) roasting chicken
Salt and freshly ground black pepper, to taste
4 tablespoons butter
1 large onion, finely chopped
2 celery stalks, finely chopped
1 pound baby collards, washed (if baby collards are not available, substitute 1 pound mature collards, stemmed, and finely julienned)
2 cups crumbled Everyday Cornbread (page 20) or other unsweetened cornbread
2 large eggs, beaten

Preheat the oven to 450°.

Wash and dry the chicken and season it inside and out with salt and pepper.

Melt the butter in a large frying pan and sauté the onion and celery over medium heat until soft and translucent. If using mature collards, add them to the pan just before the onion and celery are done and sauté for about 5 minutes, stirring frequently until they are wilted. (If you are using baby collards, you can skip this step.)

In a mixing bowl, combine the onions, celery, and greens with the crumbled cornbread and beaten egg. Mix thoroughly and season with salt and pepper.

Loosely fill the cavity of the bird with the filling. Place the chicken on a rack in a roasting pan and bake for 15 minutes. Turn the oven down to 350° and continue to cook until a thermometer inserted in the thickest part of the thigh reads 165°, about 40–50 minutes depending on the size of the chicken.

Remove the chicken from the oven, loosely cover with aluminum foil, and let stand for about 10 minutes. Remove the stuffing to a serving bowl, carve the chicken, and serve.

# Shrimp and Greens on Fried Grits

*Shrimp and grits are a Low Country tradition. The grits in this recipe are fried into crisp cakes and topped with greens and shrimp in a spicy tomato sauce. Supermarket grits, usually labeled "quick grits," will do, but if you can find stone-ground grits, by all means use them for their finer texture and flavor. Avoid anything called "instant grits." Serve these for breakfast, as a first course, or as a supper dish.*

### MAKES 8 SERVINGS

**FOR THE GRITS**

4 cups water

1 teaspoon salt

1 cup grits, stone ground if possible

**FOR THE SHRIMP AND GREENS**

4 slices bacon

1 onion, chopped

2 garlic cloves, finely chopped

½ teaspoon crushed red pepper flakes

1 (28-ounce) can whole tomatoes

1 pound collard or mustard greens, washed, stemmed, and cut into 1-inch pieces

Water or chicken stock, if needed

2 eggs, beaten

Flour for dredging

4 tablespoons olive oil or bacon fat

1 pound shrimp, peeled and deveined

Oil or bacon fat, for frying

Combine the water and salt in a large pot and bring to a boil. Slowly whisk in the grits and cook over low heat until they are as thick as cornmeal mush, about 20 minutes. Stir in more boiling water if the grits become too thick.

Pour the hot grits onto a platter or baking pan in a roughly ¾-inch-thick layer. Cover with plastic wrap and allow to cool, then refrigerate until cold.

Cut the bacon crosswise into ¼-inch strips and cook in a large frying pan until crisp. Remove the bacon, leaving the fat behind, and set aside. Add the onions and cook until soft and translucent. Add the garlic and red pepper flakes and cook until fragrant, about 30 seconds.

Crush the tomatoes with your hands, and add them and their juice to the pan; mix well. Add the greens, cover the pan, and cook until tender, about 40 minutes. (If the mixture gets too thick and threatens to stick, add a little water or chicken stock.)

While the greens are cooking, cut the grits into rectangles (or pie-shaped slices if your platter is round). Heat the oil or bacon fat in a frying pan. Dip each slice of grits into the eggs, then dredge in flour. Working in batches, fry the grits until heated through and brown and crusty on the outside. Set aside on a rack.

Add the shrimp to the greens and tomatoes and cook until the shrimp just turn pink—do not overcook. Top each of the grits cakes with some of the shrimp and greens. Serve immediately.

# Red Posole with Collard Greens

*Posole, a pork and hominy stew made with fresh roasted green chili or ground, dried red chili, is a tradition in northern New Mexico. This version is based on a recipe by Melissa Clark that appeared in the* New York Times. *Her recipe is based on one by San Francisco chef Mitchell Rosenthal. I use a slow cooker for the long simmering necessary for the flavors to develop and the hominy to become tender. Plan ahead to soak the hominy overnight.*

### MAKES 12 SERVINGS

1 pound dried hominy

4 tablespoons vegetable oil, divided

3 pounds boneless pork loin roast, cut into 1½-inch cubes

Salt and freshly ground black pepper, to taste

2 medium yellow onions, finely chopped

6 garlic cloves, chopped

1½ cups chicken stock

2 tablespoons ground Chimayo New Mexico chili or
    ancho chili (or less for less heat)

3 bay leaves

1 teaspoon ground cumin

2 tablespoons dried Mexican oregano

2 pounds collard greens, washed, stemmed, and chopped

Lime wedges, for garnish

Chopped cilantro, for garnish

Chopped avocado, for garnish

Soak the hominy in water overnight and drain.

Heat 2 tablespoons of the oil in a large frying pan. Salt and pepper the pork cubes and brown them in the hot fat in two batches, adding the remaining oil after the first batch is removed. Set the pork aside, leaving the fat in the pan.

Lower the heat, add the onions, and cook until translucent, about 10 minutes. Add the garlic and cook until fragrant, about 30 seconds. Deglaze the pan with the chicken stock, making sure to scrape up all the brown bits from the bottom of the pan. Stir in the chili, bay leaves, cumin, and oregano.

Place the hominy, pork, collard greens, and liquid from the frying pan in a slow cooker and stir to combine. Cover and cook on high for about 6 hours. Taste and add additional salt and pepper if needed.

Discard the bay leaves and serve in soup bowls, passing the garnishes separately.

# West African Greens and Peanut Stew

*Peanut stews, often called* maefe *or* maffé, *are found in the cuisines of many west and central African nations. They might be made with lamb, beef, chicken, or even fish, and often contain greens, tomatoes, and root vegetables. This rib-sticking and delicious version is made with chicken, collards, and sweet potatoes. Creamy peanut butter without added sugar saves the cook the effort of grinding the nuts. The stew is often served with rice and can be made vegetarian by leaving out the chicken and using vegetable stock.*

MAKES 4–6 SERVINGS

2 tablespoons vegetable oil

1 medium red onion, chopped

4 garlic cloves, minced

1 tablespoon ground coriander

1 teaspoon crushed red pepper flakes

3 tablespoons grated fresh ginger

1 pound skinless, boneless chicken thighs, cut into
    1-inch cubes

Salt and freshly ground black pepper, to taste

4 cups homemade chicken stock or commercial
    low-sodium chicken stock

2 sweet potatoes, peeled and cut into ½-inch cubes

1 pound collard greens, washed, stemmed, and cut into
    1-inch pieces

1 (14½-ounce) can diced fire-roasted tomatoes

1 cup creamy, no-sugar-added peanut butter

Cooked rice (optional)

⅓ cup chopped peanuts, for garnish

½ cup chopped fresh cilantro, for garnish

In a medium Dutch oven, heat the oil over medium heat and cook the onions until tender but not brown, about 8 minutes. Add the garlic, coriander, red pepper flakes, and ginger and cook until the mixture is fragrant, about 1 minute. Salt and pepper the chicken, add it to the onion and spices, and cook, stirring until lightly brown.

Add the chicken stock and the sweet potatoes. Bring to a boil, reduce the heat to a simmer, and cook until the sweet potatoes are tender, about 10–15 minutes.

Stir in the collard greens, tomatoes with their juice, and peanut butter and simmer, stirring occasionally, until the stew is thickened, about 20 minutes. Serve over rice, if desired, and garnish with peanuts and cilantro.

# Garlicky Collard Greens on Cornbread with Poached Eggs

*I had never considered greens breakfast food until I ordered chef Jamie Parry's Garlicky Greens on Toast with a Poached Egg at his restaurant, Another Fork in the Road, in Milan, New York. He used kale, but the southerner in me got me thinking, "If kale is good, wouldn't collards be even better?" And even though I love a crusty piece of toast, I couldn't resist trying it with cornbread. I think the result is pretty wonderful.*

### MAKES 4 SERVINGS

2 tablespoons olive oil

8 garlic cloves, thinly sliced

1½ pounds collard greens, washed, stemmed, and cut into chiffonade

½ teaspoon salt

½ teaspoon crushed red pepper flakes

½ cup water

1 recipe Everyday Cornbread (page 20)

8 poached eggs

In a frying pan with a lid, heat the oil over medium heat and cook the garlic until lightly brown. Add the collards, salt, and red pepper flakes. Stir until wilted. Add the water, cover, and cook until the greens are tender, about 10 minutes.

Meanwhile, preheat the broiler. Split the cornbread slices in half and toast them under the broiler until lightly brown.

Drain the collards. Cover each wedge of cornbread with a layer of collards and garlic, then top with a poached egg.

# Relishes

The South is known for its pickles and preserves. Many of them provide the acid that perks up a dish of greens. Monroe, Louisiana, chef Cory Bahr's Collard Green Marmalade is a star with both grilled and fried foods, and Bahr was kind enough to let me reproduce the recipe here. Collard kraut is remembered fondly by North Carolina cooks of an earlier generation. Making it is a process that would be difficult to embark on in most home kitchens. It's probably more practical for most of us to buy collard kraut from a company like April McGreger's Farmer's Daughter (www.farmersdaughterbrand.com).

# Chowchow

*Mike's and my favorite accompaniment for almost any kind of
greens is our home-canned chowchow. It's loosely based on a recipe
from my grandmother, although we've modified it so much that
she probably wouldn't recognize it. But I'll bet she would love its
sweet and sour spiciness. We eat it not only on greens but also on
hot dogs and as a relish for almost any other southern meal.*

MAKES 6 (½-PINT) JARS

½ head cabbage, cored and chopped

4 medium green tomatoes, chopped

2 cucumbers, peeled and chopped

2 onions, chopped

3 medium ripe tomatoes, chopped

2 bell peppers (red, yellow, or purple), chopped

¼ cup salt

¾ cup brown sugar

1 garlic clove, sliced

2 tablespoons mustard seeds

½ tablespoon celery seed

½ tablespoon red pepper flakes

1 tablespoon grated fresh ginger

1 tablespoon powdered turmeric

4 bay leaves

Apple cider vinegar

Mix the chopped vegetables with the salt and let stand overnight. Using a kitchen towel, wring the moisture out of the vegetables.

In a large stockpot or Dutch oven, combine the vegetables with the remaining ingredients except the vinegar, then add enough vinegar to cover the mixture by ¼ inch. Bring to a boil and simmer for 10 minutes. Remove from the heat and reserve the garlic and bay leaves.

Sterilize 6 half-pint jars by immersing them in boiling water for 10 minutes or heating them in a 200° oven for 20 minutes.

Fill the hot jars with the mixture, garnishing with the garlic and bay leaves. Seal the jars with rings and lids and process in a boiling water bath for 15 minutes to insure a proper seal. Let the jars sit for two weeks in a cool, dark place to allow flavors to develop. Refrigerate after opening.

# Collard Greens Marmalade

*Cory Bahr is owner and chef of Restaurant Cotton, located in an old cotton warehouse on the Ouachita River in his (and my) hometown of Monroe, Louisiana. Dedicated to proving that "there's good cooking in Louisiana outside New Orleans," Bahr carefully sources local ingredients and cooks them in imaginative ways. Examples include his prize-winning North Louisiana Bouillabaisse and this delicious marmalade, which is equally at home with fried seafood or on a sandwich.*

### MAKES 1 QUART

---

½ cup roughly chopped bacon (10–12 slices)

2 medium yellow onions, thinly sliced

1 tablespoon mustard seeds

1 teaspoon crushed red pepper flakes

4 garlic cloves, thinly sliced

1 jalapeño pepper, seeds removed, thinly sliced

1 teaspoon crushed red pepper flakes

1 pound collard greens, washed, stemmed, and roughly chopped

1½ cups sugar

1½ cups water

1½ cups apple cider vinegar

Salt and freshly ground black pepper, to taste

---

In a large frying pan over medium heat render the bacon. Remove and drain on paper towels, leaving the fat in the pan. Add the onions and lightly brown them over medium-high heat, about 5–7 minutes. Add the mustard seeds, red pepper flakes, garlic, and jalapeños. Continue cooking for about 3 minutes.

Toss in the collard greens and stir to combine. Add the sugar, water, and vinegar and reduce, over medium-high heat, to a thickened, syrupy consistency, about half an hour. Season with salt and pepper. Cool to room temperature and store in the refrigerator in a tightly sealed container for up to one month, or follow standard canning procedures for longer storage.

# Cucumber and Onion Relish

*Peggy Dean Bowman-Belcher, a lifelong resident of Dinwiddie County, near Petersburg, Virginia, makes this cucumber and onion relish as an accompaniment to collards. The recipe came from her parents and other older residents of the county. She also uses the relish with cabbage, fresh string beans, and other vegetables. There's no hot pepper in this relish, she says, because she adds pepper when cooking the collards.*

MAKES 1–2 CUPS

---

½ English cucumber, peeled and thinly sliced
½ Vidalia or other sweet onion, thinly sliced
Apple cider vinegar
Cold water
Salt, to taste

---

In a small bowl, combine the cucumber and onion with vinegar to cover. Add a splash of cold water to cut the acidity of the vinegar. Season with salt and refrigerate. Serve cold.

# Pickled Mustard Greens

*Asians are masters of the art of pickling and use varieties of greens not easily found in this country outside Asian markets, but our ordinary mustard greens lend themselves very well to this Asian-inspired treatment. Use them on hot dogs or alongside any other meat or vegetable dish that could benefit from a tart, spicy relish. We think they're a perfect foil for the sweetness of cooked tomato dishes.*

MAKES 1 QUART

½ cup apple cider vinegar

1 cup cold water

1 tablespoon kosher salt

2 tablespoons sugar

1 teaspoon black mustard seeds

2 teaspoons yellow mustard seeds

1 pound mustard greens, washed, stemmed, and cut into
   1-inch pieces

4 garlic cloves, sliced

2 red jalapeño peppers or other hot pepper, seeded and sliced

Sterilize a 1-quart jar by immersing it in boiling water for 10 minutes or heating it in a 200° oven for 20 minutes.

Bring the vinegar, water, salt, sugar, and mustard seeds to a boil in a medium saucepan.

Pack the mustard greens into the jar, interspersing them with the garlic and jalapeños. Pour the hot vinegar mixture over the greens, cover the jar, and refrigerate for 2–3 days before serving.

# Acknowledgments

First of all, I would like to thank Elaine Maisner and the staff at the UNC Press. Elaine encouraged me to write this book, gave me invaluable editorial advice, and answered my often naïve questions with unfailing good nature. Leni Sorensen kindly gave me a crash course on the foodways and culinary history of the South, threw in gardening tips, fed me her delicious homemade tamales, and sent me on my way with three dozen eggs from her chickens. I also owe a great debt to Adrian Miller and John T Edge for their scholarship and supportive friendship, and to Professor Edward H. Davis and Professor Chris Gunter for answering questions about regional consumption of greens.

Many friends and talented chefs have talked greens and shared recipes with me. These include Cory Bahr, Liz Barron, Susan Blue, Peggy Dean Bowman-Belcher, Sandra Gutierrez, Donald Goodman, Emmilee Green, Alex Harrell, Andy Holtzman and Michael Mele, Kym Lucas and Mark Retherford, Angie Mosier, Scott Mun, Elizabeth Petty, Simone Rathle, and Tony Towler.

And finally, I would like to thank Mike Cavanagh, without whom this book would not have been possible.

# Index

Printed in the USA
CPSIA information can be obtained
at www.ICGtesting.com
CBHW042117260424
7639CB00007B/258